Itching Ears

How the most important biblical doctrines
are based on a foundation of Genesis

By Paul F. Taylor

*For the time will come when they will not endure sound
doctrine, but according to their own desires, because they
have itching ears, they will heap up for themselves
teachers; and they will turn their ears away from the truth,
and be turned aside to fables.*

2 Timothy 4:3-4

Just Six Days Publishing

Published by:
J6D Publications
8141 Ackerman Drive
Pensacola, FL, 32514
USA

First published in the UK in 2010 by J6D Publications, 9 Parnell Close, Littlethorpe, Leicestershire, LE19 2JS, UK
Third edition published 2014 by J6D Publications, 8141 Ackerman drive, Pensacola, FL 32514, USA

ISBN: 978-1499638196

Printed by Create Space

Acknowledgements

Thanks are due to Andy McIntosh and John Mackay for reading through the manuscript. Although they suggested corrections, it should be noted that any errors of substance or style which still remain are my fault. Thanks also to Neil Seeds, who made several helpful style suggestions when the proof version came out. Also, thanks to my son, Adam Taylor, who did a considerable amount of the research required for each chapter. Most thanks are due to my family and especially my wife, Geri, for patience and perseverance with me.

Contents

Introduction

Theory and Practice

There seems to have developed a lack of seriousness about the teachings and doctrines from the Bible in the early part of the 21st Century. Doctrine has become a despised word. I once heard a preacher declare, to appreciative murmurings from the congregation: "Aren't you glad that God didn't save you for doctrine". Of course God didn't save us for doctrine. But the purpose of doctrine is to keep our understanding on track, and to understand God better, so surely any normal Christian would want to know more about his God and Savior! But the very phrasing used by the preacher was not there to book dissent. It was to be assumed that doctrine is not only a dirty word, but a dangerous concept - a cold philosophy designed to take the Christian away from the love of and worship for Jesus.

Rick Warren, the author of *The Purpose-Driven*™ *Church*, said "The trouble with the church today is that we know too much and do little"[1] Once again, the implication is that what we know is not of value compared to what we do. There might be many who nod their heads solemnly at such comments. Yet, without a knowledge of who God is, what He is like and what He wants, our behavior as Christians remains uninformed.

One refrain that we often hear is "doctrine divides, but love unites". The problem is that this phrase does not occur anywhere in the Bible. That is because it isn't true. True love will unite, but the sort of love which attempts to paper over all differences, pretending that they don't exist, will not. And, unfortunately, the Bible also makes clear that there are some sort of divisions which we need to have. For example, in Galatians 1:8, Paul says "even if we, or an angel from heaven, preach any other gospel to you than what we have preached to you, let him be accursed." And in 2 Corinthians 6:17, Paul quotes from Isaiah, saying "Come out from among them and be separate, says the Lord." The modern ecumenical

---

[1] Rick Warren, speaking at the *Desiring God* conference, 2010

spirit suggests that we can all be together by ignoring our differences and tolerating everything. Such an idea is, however, itself a doctrine! It is actually a doctrine to say that differences of opinion don't matter and should be tolerated. It will also be noted that the one group of people who cannot be tolerated under such a regime are those who say that the Bible is true.

The apostle Paul wrote two letters to Timothy, who seems to have been a sort of protégé of Paul. In 1 Timothy 4, Paul instructs Timothy to be careful about two things.

> Watch your life and doctrine closely. Persevere in them, because if you do, you will save both yourself and your hearers. (1 Timothy 4:16, NIV)

Timothy is instructed to watch his life and his doctrine. Of course, the way that Timothy lives is important. It is a poor witness, if we live a life that is dishonoring to God. So, clearly, *orthopraxy* (correct practice or behaviour) is very important. But *orthodoxy* is equally important. Timothy is to watch his doctrine.

Why? Because by so doing people will be saved. Orthodoxy without orthopraxy is dead. But orthopraxy without orthodoxy is useless. Paul has more to say on this matter in his second epistle.

> I charge you therefore before God and the Lord Jesus Christ, who will judge the living and the dead at His appearing and His kingdom: Preach the word! Be ready in season and out of season. Convince, rebuke, exhort, with all longsuffering and teaching. For the time will come when they will not endure sound doctrine, but according to their own desires, because they have itching ears, they will heap up for themselves teachers; and they will turn their ears away from the truth, and be turned aside to fables. But you be watchful in all things, endure afflictions, do the work of an evangelist, fulfill your ministry. (2 Timothy 4:1-5)

This passage contains an important prophecy - "the time will come when they will not endure sound doctrine". Who are "they"? They are the sort of people, to whom Timothy is speaking. Timothy was being sent to pastor churches. So the people who will not endure sound doctrine are people in churches. In the passage from 1 Timothy, Paul said that doctrine was part of ensuring that people were saved. In 2 Timothy, he expands on this matter. The consequences of not having sound doctrine are that the people will "turn their ears away from the truth and be turned aside to fables". Whereas Timothy's work in teaching sound doctrine was to be a major part of his "work of an evangelist" - so the preaching of the Gospel was to involve sound doctrine..

Paul's exhortation to Timothy was basically to postpone the day when sound doctrine would not be endured. He was to "Preach the word! Be ready in season and out of season. Convince, rebuke, exhort, with all longsuffering and teaching." The word translated "teaching" is translated as "doctrine" in the KJV, and comes from precisely the same root as the other occasion in this passage when the word doctrine is used. That is the measure of the forcefulness, with which Paul requires Timothy to present doctrine. There is an urgency in the passage. Timothy is to teach doctrine, because there will be a time when he will not be able to. By implication, the church today is to teach doctrine, because there will come a time when it will not be possible. That time seems to be largely upon us today.

I saw a bumper sticker on a car. It read "they will know we are Christians by our love", which is a line from a song, not from the Bible. The Bible actually says "you will know them by their fruits" (Matthew 7:16) - and this applies not just to Christians, but also to knowing who the false teachers are. But on this sticker, it actually read "they will know we are Christians by our doctrine", with the word "doctrine" crossed out and replaced with "love". The implication, as above, is that love and doctrine are mutually exclusive. If you are interested in doctrine, you are not interested in love. Loving people are not interested in doctrine.

These are the sort of people described in that memorable phrase by Paul as having "itching ears". Such people will find themselves teachers, who will reinforce their desire not to have doctrine. They are teachers who do not love doctrine! They are teachers

who don't teach. Such teachers are themselves the
punishment for the unbelief of their hearers. Paul's
strong implication is that such teachers will lead their
listeners, not to salvation, but to destruction. Paul
makes clear to Timothy that his adherence to good
teaching or doctrine is not optional. Paul says "I
charge you!"

Of course, Paul actually says "I charge you
therefore...". The *therefore* implies that the reason for
this charge, to teach doctrine, is what Paul has said in
the previous chapter. In 2 Timothy 3, Paul has said:

> Evil men and impostors will grow worse and worse,
> deceiving and being deceived. But you must
> continue in the things which you have learned and
> been assured of, knowing from whom you have
> learned them, and that from childhood you have
> known the Holy Scriptures, which are able to
> make you wise for salvation through faith which is
> in Christ Jesus. All Scripture is given by inspiration
> of God, and is profitable for doctrine, for reproof,
> for correction, for instruction in righteousness,

that the man of God may be complete, thoroughly equipped for every good work. (2 Timothy 3:13-17)

The sort of people, therefore, who teach such false doctrines are "evil men and imposters". What is more, they "will grow worse and worse". So Timothy is exhorted to "continue in the things which you have learned". What are these things? They are the Holy Scriptures. Today, we can apply the knowledge of the Holy Scriptures to the entire Bible. I have written elsewhere about how the concept of the canon of Scripture applies to the New Testament as well as the Old, but not to extra-biblical books such as the apocrypha.[2] Brian Edwards has written what I consider to be the best evocation of this position.[3] At the time of Paul writing his epistle, however, the Scripture that he refers to must be the Old Testament. These Old Testament scriptures begin with, and are founded upon, the book of Genesis.

---

[2] Taylor, P., *Is the Bible Enough?* In Ham, K. (ed.) (2008) *New Answers Book 2*, (Green Forest, AR: Master Books)

[3] Edwards, B.H., *Why 66?* In Ham, K. (ed.) (2008) *New Answers Book 2*, (Green Forest, AR: Master Books)

Which Doctrines are Important?

There is a sense in which this question is redundant. All doctrines are important. Nevertheless, it must be admitted that some doctrines are more important than others. Can we rank the doctrine of the Trinity alongside my assertion that baptism is to be by immersion and for believers only? I would suggest not. I cannot have fellowship with someone who disagrees on the Trinity, but I can have fellowship with a Bible-believing evangelical, who believes that baptism can be appropriate for infants. And how do these doctrines compare with teachings on our modes of worship?

Three Point Scale of Doctrines

I have not come across any other comment on the relative rankings of doctrines, like the one that I am about to use. But I like to classify doctrines as Primary, Secondary and Tertiary.

Primary Doctrines are essential indicators of orthodoxy. Without an acceptance of these doctrines, the subject is outside of the church and therefore outside of fellowship. To clarify this point, a new

Christian may not have got all their doctrine straight, and might, for example, not fully understand the concept of the Trinity (and none of us *fully* understand it!). But when such a primary doctrine is explained, if the subject consistently rejects it, and says they cannot accept it, one must doubt whether they have really been saved at all. If such a doctrine is a primary doctrine, then the Holy Spirit will witness to people that the doctrine is true. Examples of primary doctrines are the ones on which I focus in this book.

Secondary Doctrines are not unimportant. A church ought to take an official position on such a doctrine. But in joint church initiatives it ought to be possible to work with people who do not share these doctrines. For example, I hinted above that I hold to the doctrine of Believers' Baptism by immersion. Not everyone who works for a ministry, like the one for which I work, will necessarily agree with me on this. Christian ministries may not be able to take a position on such a secondary doctrine. But my church **does** take a position on this, and it should. Other examples of secondary doctrines would be Calvinism vs. Arminianism, or differing eschatological positions, or what position one takes on the Baptism into the Holy Spirit.

Tertiary Doctrines are those, on which people even within a church will differ. Such doctrines would include how the Sunday School should be taught, or different modes of worship music.

This book can only concentrate on Primary Doctrines, and does not even cover all of these! However, one of the Primary Doctrines is not listed as a chapter heading. It is the doctrine of biblical creationism - that the Genesis account is one of literal history. Many, many Christians assume that the issue of creationism is a secondary doctrine. Can I justify placing it as a primary? I believe I can. Of course, it is possible to be saved without believing in 6-day creationism. The point is that such a belief impinges on a belief in the authority and inerrancy of scripture. It is part of the purpose of this book to show that failure to believe in Genesis leads to a weak view of inerrancy and therefore a lack of authority for any of the other doctrines. It is the contention of this book that all Christian doctrines are founded on a foundation of Genesis.

Let me explain how this principle outworks in practice. I will make no comment on where I stand on the Calvinism/Arminianism divide. One usually hears from godly people on both sides that they accept one another as Bible-believing Christians, even though they differ on this point. In practice, however, Christians on both sides often find difficulty in fellowshipping together in parachurch ministries. Yet Christians on both sides will often find it easy to fellowship with someone from the same side, even if that other person disagrees that Genesis should be taken as literal.

For example, I once used this analogy to a conference almost entirely made up of Calvinists. Person A is a Calvinist who believes Genesis in a 6-day creation, as Genesis teaches.. Person B is a Calvinist, who believes in long day-ages. Person C is an Arminian who believes in a 6-day creation. My challenge to Person A is "who do you find it easier to have fellowship with"? In practice, it will usually be Person B - and I have no doubt that a similar scenario put to an Arminian would provoke an analogous response. My argument is that Person A should have more in common with Person C. That is because the issue of the truth of Genesis is a primary doctrine, but Calvinism vs. Arminianism is secondary.

There are many who will struggle with that last concept - and might struggle even more if I had used cessationism/pentecostalism as the secondary divide. What I want to convince you of, gentle reader, is that the secondary issues are held by sincere people, who equally believe the Bible to be true, but differ on the interpretation of certain passages. But the disagreement on Genesis is not between different interpretations. It is between those who interpret Genesis, and those who simply read what it plainly says. The secondary doctrines have arisen because some passages of scripture are hard to get a handle on. Differing views of Genesis have built up, because there are those who understand perfectly well what Genesis actually says, but use extra-biblical filters, such as evolution, millions of years or the Big Bang, as an authority over and above the plain reading.

No Time for Itching Ears

This book, therefore, is a plea for a return to the love of sound doctrine. It is a plea it recognize that Genesis is the foundation of all Christian doctrine, and that such doctrine is important and essential. If the time will come - and, indeed, I am of the opinion that it has already come - when they will not endure sound doctrine, then this book is a plea to reverse that trend. The need for sound doctrine is great. This is no time for itching ears!

Genesis and the Trinity

I believe in the Trinity

OK, you Christians – hands up all those who believe in the Trinity! That's a lot of hands, I'm pleased to see. Mind you, some of your hands are a bit shaky, and some of you have only put your hands up very tentatively, as if you are worried that I might pounce on one of you and ask you to explain the Trinity. For instance, you sir... that's right, the gentleman who is trying to hide behind the pillar. You seem to believe in the Trinity – well, your hand is half up, so maybe you believe in a one-point-five-nity. Sorry, I can't quite hear you. Perhaps I'd better ask everyone. Hands up those who can explain the Trinity to me! There's a lot fewer hands now. Perhaps if I asked you again whether or not you believed in the Trinity, there would be fewer hands.

You sir! Yes, you, on the back row, looking round to see if there is someone behind you! How would you explain the Trinity? St Patrick? A three-leafed shamrock? Actually, that does make some sense. It is really one leaf, but we can see three bits to it. The Trinity is deeper than that though.

I know I seem to be bullying you, and perhaps that's not quite fair at this pastors' conference, but I really think we need to know our stuff here. Do we actually believe the Trinity? In fact, is it really that important? We hear that it is not just Unitarians these days who don't believe in the Trinity. We know that Jehovah's Witnesses don't, either. Oneness Pentecostals don't believe in the Trinity, though they do, surprisingly, believe that Jesus is God and that the Holy Spirit is God as well as believing that the Father is God. They just don't believe they are God at the same time. That's a simplification of their view, I know, and we'll explain their view (and why it is wrong) later. But for now, we'll emphasize that Oneness Pentecostals do not believe in the Trinity.[1]

---

[1] There are a number of denominations or groupings that would be classed as Oneness Pentecostals. Their names can be confusing. For example, there is a church known as the New Apostolic Church, which is, as far as I know, a Oneness church. However, the Apostolic Church (UK) declares itself on its website to be a Trinitarian church, and is therefore a Classical

Now, however, we hear that there are ministers within established denominations – Baptists, Methodists, Anglicans etc. - who do not believe in the Trinity. What a mix up! So maybe it is important to know where we stand.

Athanasius certainly thought so. Haven't you heard of Athanasius? What about you Anglicans? The 1662 Book of Common Prayer contains the Athanasian Creed, does it not? What? You never use that creed? You just use the Apostles Creed and the Nicene Creed. Yes, they are good, but you are missing a treat if you don't use the Athanasian Creed.

Yes, I know that some people don't believe the Athanasian Creed was written by Athanasius[2]. It doesn't really matter. The Creed definitely sums up Athanasius's views - and the views of the church at that time. Athanasius was arguing with the Arians,

---

Pentecostal Church. I was once a member of an Apostolic Church (UK) fellowship. Confused? If in doubt, check their statements of faith.

[2] **Athanasian Creed**. (2009). In *Encyclopædia Britannica*. Retrieved October 22, 2009, from Encyclopædia Britannica Online: http://www.britannica.com/EBchecked/topic/40585/Athanasian-Creed

who believed that Jesus could not be of one substance with the Father, because the Father is immutable, whereas Jesus must have changed as He grew. They didn't realize that these differences are differences of *personhood*, not deity. We need to read the Athanasian Creed again, because it is such a masterful statement of the doctrines of the Trinity and the Hypostatic Union (which we'll look at in chapter 2).

The Athanasian Creed is set out below.

> Whosoever will be saved, before all things it is necessary that he hold the catholic[3] faith. Which faith except everyone do keep whole and undefiled, without doubt he shall perish everlastingly. And the catholic faith is this: That we worship one God in Trinity, and Trinity in Unity, neither confounding the persons, nor dividing the substance.
>
> For there is one Person of the Father, another of the Son, and another of the Holy Spirit. But the godhead of the Father, of the Son, and of the Holy

---

[3] By using the term 'catholic', Athanasian means 'the universal church'. He is not referring to the Roman Catholic Church.

Spirit, is all one, the glory equal, the majesty co-eternal.

Such as the Father is, such is the Son, and such is the Holy Spirit. The Father uncreated, the Son uncreated, and the Holy Spirit uncreated. The Father incomprehensible, the Son incomprehensible, and the Holy Spirit incomprehensible.

The Father eternal, the Son eternal, and the Holy Spirit eternal. And yet they are not three eternals, but one Eternal.

As also there are not three incomprehensibles, nor three uncreated, but one Uncreated, and one Incomprehensible. So likewise the Father is Almighty, the Son Almighty, and the Holy Spirit Almighty. And yet they are not three almighties, but one Almighty.

So the Father is God, the Son is God, and the Holy Spirit is God. And yet they are not three gods, but one God.

So likewise the Father is Lord, the Son Lord, and the Holy Spirit Lord. And yet not three lords, but one Lord.

For as we are compelled by the Christian verity to acknowledge each Person by Himself to be both God and Lord, so we are also forbidden by the catholic religion to say that there are three gods or three lords.

The Father is made of none, neither created, nor begotten. The Son is of the Father alone, not made, nor created, but begotten. The Holy Spirit is of the Father, neither made, nor created, nor begotten, but proceeding.

So there is one Father, not three fathers; one Son, not three sons; one Holy Spirit, not three holy spirits.

And in the Trinity none is before or after another; none is greater or less than another, but all three Persons are co-eternal together and co-equal. So that in all things, as is aforesaid, the Unity in Trinity and the Trinity in Unity is to be worshipped.

He therefore that will be saved must think thus of the Trinity.

Furthermore, it is necessary to everlasting salvation that he also believe rightly the Incarnation of our Lord Jesus Christ. For the right faith is, that we believe and confess, that our Lord Jesus Christ, the Son of God, is God and man; God, of the substance of the Father, begotten before the worlds; and man of the substance of his mother, born in the world; perfect God and perfect man, of a rational soul and human flesh subsisting. Equal to the Father, as touching His godhead; and inferior to the Father, as touching His manhood; who, although He is God and man, yet he is not two, but one Christ; one, not by conversion of the godhead into flesh but by taking of the manhood into God; one altogether; not by confusion of substance, but by unity of person. For as the rational soul and flesh is one man, so God and man is one Christ; who suffered for our salvation, descended into hell, rose again the third day from the dead. He ascended into heaven, He sits at the right hand of the Father, God Almighty, from whence He will come to judge the quick and the dead. At His coming all men will rise again with their bodies and shall give account for their own works. And they that have done good shall go into life everlasting; and they that have done evil into everlasting fire.

This is the catholic faith, which except a man believe faithfully, he cannot be saved.[4]

So the Athanasian Creed is emphasizing that, as far as Athanasius is concerned, belief in the doctrine of the Trinity is necessary for salvation. Let's be clear on this – when you are saved you don't have to believe everything right straight away. But, nevertheless, the doctrine of the Trinity is being described as an essential doctrine, so it is something you need to come to grips with early in your Christian walk. On our three point scale of doctrines, it is in the Primary category. (see introduction, p9)

[4] **Athanasian Creed** (500AD). From *Christian Apologetics and Research Ministry*. Retrieved October 22, 2009, from: http://www.carm.org/christianity/creeds-and-confessions/athanasian-creed-500-ad

What does it mean?

In this book, we will be looking at these doctrines in three ways.

1. What does it mean?

2. Where is it found in the Bible?

3. Is it rooted in Genesis?

There have been many books, sermons and presentations over the centuries which have dealt with the doctrine of the Trinity. Lots of helpful analogies have been developed. However, it needs to be emphasized that none of these analogies really fully encapsulates the correctness of the doctrine of the Trinity, as stated in the Athanasian Creed.

One of the most famous analogies used is ascribed to Patrick of Ireland (although there are many who claim that he actually came from Wales[5]). Patrick apparently thought it was necessary to tell pagans in the island of Ireland about the Trinity, in order to emphasize the importance of believing Jesus to be the Son of God. In

[5] **Welsh Village Claims St Patrick**, from BBC online, Retrieved October 22, 2009, from: http://news.bbc.co.uk/1/hi/wales/south_west/3520656.stm

doing so, he is traditionally thought to have used a shamrock as an analogy for the Trinity, because it is a three leafed plant, with only one stalk[6].

There are many similar analogies to this, and, while they can be helpful, it is probably best not to push them too far. God is not three separate leaves on a single stalk, but at least the analogy can help us to see that there is both unity and threeness in the concept of God. It is clear that the doctrine of the Trinity was important to Patrick and to those who followed him. Though the famous hymn, St Patrick's Breastplate, is unlikely to have been written directly by Patrick, it is probably a reasonable summary of his ideas.

[6] **Saint Patrick**. (2009). In *Encyclopædia Britannica*. Retrieved October 22, 2009, from Encyclopædia Britannica Online: http://www.britannica.com/EBchecked/topic/446636/Saint-Patrick

I bind unto myself the Name,
The strong Name of the Trinity,
By invocation of the same,
The Three in One and One in Three.
By Whom all nature hath creation,
Eternal Father, Spirit, Word:
Praise to the Lord of my salvation,
Salvation is of Christ the Lord[7].

Perhaps more accurate would be the famous Trinity theological diagram, reproduced below.

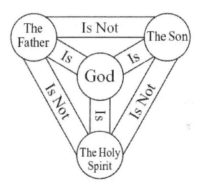

The doctrine lists each person of the Trinity at a corner of a triangle. The word 'God' (Latin 'Deus') is at the center of the triangle, with each person linked by

[7] **St Patrick's Breastplate**, (final verse), translated 1889, Cecil Alexander, Cyber Hymnal, retrieved October 22, 2009, http://www.cyberhymnal.org/htm/s/t/stpatric.htm

the word 'Est' – 'Is'. The diagram is emphasizing that the Father is God, the Son is God and the Holy Spirit is God, but that there is one God. The diagram also emphasizes that the Father is not the Son or the Holy Spirit, the Son is not the Father or the Holy Spirit and the Holy Spirit is not the Son or the Father. Thus there are three persons yet one God. The word person is used because each person is able to interact and to be self-aware, even though there is one God.

Before we look for the scriptural justification for such a doctrine, I can pursue this bunny trail. Maybe the sheer complexity of the doctrine paradoxically illustrates its truthfulness. No other religion uses such a doctrine[8].

There is only one God

It is a mistake to believe that Trinitarianism implies polytheism – or, rather, tritheism. The Trinity is specifically not a doctrine of three gods, as some suppose. Two passages in the Quran suggest an

---

[8] Some have noted a version of trinity in various religions, such as Mithraism. This will be analysed later, and seen to be completely different from the Christian, biblical doctrine of the Trinity.

opposition to Trinitarian doctrine, but actually it is an opposition to a doctrine of tritheism.

> O followers of the Book! do not exceed the limits in your religion, and do not speak (lies) against Allah, but (speak) the truth; the Messiah, Isa son of Marium is only an apostle of Allah and His Word which He communicated to Marium and a spirit from Him; believe therefore in Allah and His apostles, and say not, Three. Desist, it is better for you; Allah is only one Allah; far be It from His glory that He should have a son, whatever is in the heavens and whatever is in the earth is His, and Allah is sufficient for a Protector. [Sura 4:171]

> Certainly they disbelieve who say: Surely Allah is the third (person) of the three; and there is no god but the one Allah, and if they desist not from what they say, a painful chastisement shall befall those among them who disbelieve. [Sura 5:73][9]

Although these verses specifically rule out Trinitarianism, or the idea that Jesus (referred to as Isa in the Quran) was God, it is likely that Mohammed had

[9] **Quran (Shakir, English)**, *Online Quran Project*, Retrieved October 22, 2009, http://al-quran.info

come across a pseudo-Christian heretical cult, which believed, not in a Trinity, but a tritheist grouping of God, Jesus and Mary. This sect could possibly have been the Collyridian sect, who worshipped Mary as a goddess[10]. Whether the Quran was opposing tritheism or Trinitarianism is not an important point, however, because the first quoted verse above contradicts the deity of Jesus, and can therefore be used to oppose either tritheism or Trinitarianism. We shall more to say, in passing, on Sura 4:171, in the chapter on the *hypostatic union.*

The reason for the brief bunny trail into Islam was as a precursor to pointing out that the Bible, too, is firmly against tritheism, or any form of polytheism.

The Old Testament clearly tells us that there is only one God.

> "You are My witnesses,"says the LORD, "And My servant whom I have chosen, That you may now and believe Me, And understand that I am He.

[10] **Collyridianism**, (2009), *Wikipedia*, Retrieved October 22, 2009, http://en.wikipedia.org/wiki/Choloridians (note that Wikipedia articles are likely to change rapidly)

Before Me there was no God formed, Nor shall there be after Me."(Isaiah 43:10)

I *am* the LORD, and *there is* no other; *There is* no God besides Me. I will gird you, though you have not known Me. (Isaiah 45:5)

The book of Isaiah is full of instances, like the above, where we are told:

1. That the LORD is God.

2. That there is no other God.

3. That there was no God before God, and will be no God to replace Him afterwards.

The New Testament reiterates the point about there being only one God.

For even if there are so-called gods, whether in heaven or on earth (as there are many gods and many lords), yet for us *there is* one God, the Father, of whom *are* all things, and we for Him; and one Lord Jesus Christ, through whom *are* all things, and through whom we *live.* (1 Corinthians 8:5-6)

But then, indeed, when you did not know God, you served those which by nature are not gods. But now after you have known God, or rather are known by God, how *is it that* you turn again to the weak and beggarly elements, to which you desire again to be in bondage? (Galatians 4:8-9)

This is the first step in understanding the doctrine of the Trinity – to realize how firmly the Bible establishes that there is only one God. Notice also that the above passages make clear that there is no other God beside God. The passage in 1 Corinthians adds that there are many so-called gods, who are not real gods. That means that any other god we might come across is a false god or counterfeit god – an idol. It is therefore demonic. It is demonic even if it happens to bear the same name in an alternative religion to the true God of the Bible. If the attributes of that god are not the same as the true God, then it is demonic. For that reason, we can deduce that Allah is not the same as our God. The attributes associated to Allah are different from those of God. We will see later the importance of believing in the Son, but we note from the Quranic passages above that Allah has no son. God does have a Son, therefore Allah is not God; Allah is demonic. This sounds harsh, but it is the conclusion of the Bible, not the conclusion of fallible people.

It is important to start our doctrine of the Trinity at this point, otherwise our doctrine will be tritheism, rather than the Trinity. Trinity comes from a Latin term, but we can see its roots even in English; *tri + unity*. It is only when we have established the *unity* part of the equation that we will really be able to emphasize the threeness.

There are three persons; Father, Son and Holy Spirit

Under this heading, we are not going to get straight to the most controversial point, which is to equate all three of these terms to God Himself. Rather, our purpose at the moment is to establish that the Bible refers to Father, Son and Holy Spirit. In later paragraphs, we will see that all are described as God – but for now, let us note that these descriptions are there, and that other pseudo-Christian groups recognize the labels, though they define them differently. For example, many non-trinitarian groups can still refer to Jesus as the Son of God. They simply do not believe that the term Son of God implies divinity. Jehovah's Witnesses (JWs) would be in this camp, agreeing with Christians that Jesus is the Son of God, but disagreeing that He is actually God. JWs also accept the existence of the Holy Spirit, but think that He is simply an impersonal force. Oneness Pentecostals, on the other hand, do accept that Jesus is God, and that the Holy Spirit is God – but they maintain that, rather than a Trinity, God is simply manifest in different forms on different occasions.

The Father is God

There is very little argument on this point. Even non-Trinitarians usually agree that the Father is God. They would usually put it that God is often described as the Father. There might not seem to be much point in extending this section, therefore, except for the following point – if we can establish some of the divine ways that the title Father is used for the First Person of the Trinity, and we find the same sort of attributions for the Son and the Holy Spirit, then we lend support to the proposition that the Bible describes God as Trinity.

> Grace to you and peace from God our Father and the Lord Jesus Christ. (Philippians 1:2)

> But now, O LORD, You *are* our Father; We *are* the clay, and You our potter; And all we *are* the work of Your hand. (Isaiah 64:8)

Verses from both Old and New Testaments here describe God as Father. Moreover, the Isaiah passage describes God as Creator. We will see similar descriptions of the Son and Holy Spirit.

> But will God indeed dwell on the earth? Behold, heaven and the heaven of heavens cannot contain You. How much less this temple which I have built! (1 Kings 8:27)

> For if our heart condemns us, God is greater than our heart, and knows all things. (1 John 3:20)

These latter two verses show that God is omnipresent (everywhere) and omniscient (all-knowing).

The Son is God

Now we will look at the same attributes, to see if the Son has these descriptions.

> In the beginning was the Word, and the Word was with God, and the Word was God. (John 1:1)

The Word is being described as God, as well as with God. The Jehovah's Witnesses have a different view, translating the final phrase as "the Word was a god". Interestingly, their own publication, the *Kingdom Interlinear Greek-English Bible*, does not have the indefinite article, so confirms that the Word was "God", not just a "god".

When we compare John 1:1 with John 1:14, we see that the person being referred to as "the Word" is, in fact, Jesus.

> And the Word became flesh and dwelt among us, and we beheld His glory, the glory as of the only begotten of the Father, full of grace and truth. (John 1:14).

Genesis and the Trinity

Jesus is also here described as the "only begotten", which makes it clear that He is the Son of God.

Jesus is described as Creator in John 1:3 and Colossians 1:15-17.

> All things were made through Him, and without Him nothing was made that was made. (John 1:3)

> He (Jesus) is the image of the invisible God, the firstborn over all creation. For by Him all things were created that are in heaven and that are on earth, visible and invisible, whether thrones or dominions or principalities or powers. All things were created through Him and for Him. And He is before all things, and in Him all things consist. (Colossians 1:15-17)

Although during His time on Earth, Jesus would appear to have limited Himself to His human body, this limitation was removed after His resurrection, so that He could claim to be anywhere that was necessary. For example:

> Let this mind be in you which was also in Christ Jesus, who, being in the form of God, did not

consider it robbery to be equal with God, but made Himself of no reputation, taking the form of a bondservant, and coming in the likeness of men. (Ephesians 2:5-7)

Then Jesus said to them, "Do not be afraid. Go *and* tell My brethren to go to Galilee, and there they will see Me." (Matthew 28:10)

Now we are sure that You know all things, and have no need that anyone should question You. By this we believe that You came forth from God. (John 16:30)

The passage from John 16:30 has the disciples acknowledging that Jesus knew all things – therefore He was omniscient. Peter states that Jesus knows all things in John 21:17.

Much more can be said about the divinity of Jesus – and more will be reported on this subject in the chapter on the Incarnation. One final; point will suffice for the present study. Jesus accepted worship. The disciples in the boat worshipped Him (Matthew 14:33), and a man healed from blindness worshipped

Him (John 9:38). The last reference is particularly pertinent, written as it was by the apostle John. In Revelation, John is so taken by the power of an angel, that he twice attempts to worship the angel, but is prevented from doing so[11]. If Jesus had not considered Himself as God, He would not have accepted these acts of worship. The fact that He accepted worship is further evidence that He was and is God.

The Holy Spirit is God

> But Peter said, "Ananias, why has Satan filled your heart to lie to the Holy Spirit and keep back *part* of the price of the land for yourself? While it remained, was it not your own? And after it was sold, was it not in your own control? Why have you conceived this thing in your heart? You have not lied to men but to God." (Acts 5:3-4)

Peter says two things to Ananias about lying. First, he says that Ananias has lied to the Holy Spirit. Second, he says that he has lied to God. This only makes sense, if we accept that the Holy Spirit is God.

---

[11] Revelation 19:10 and Revelation 22:8-9

The Holy Spirit had His part to play in creation. In Genesis 1:2, we read: "And the Spirit of God was hovering over the face of the waters."Job remarked "The Spirit of God has made me." (Job 33:4). He also stated "By His Spirit He adorned the heavens." (Job 22:13). If there is one God, but we have seen that the Father, Son and Spirit are all described as the Creator, then the Father, Son and Spirit are all one God – the Trinity.

The Spirit is similarly omnipresent and omniscient, like the Father and the Son.

> Where can I go from Your Spirit? Or where can I flee from Your presence? If I ascend into heaven, You *are* there; If I make my bed in hell, behold, You *are there. If* I take the wings of the morning, And dwell in the uttermost parts of the sea, Even there Your hand shall lead me, And Your right hand shall hold me. (Psalm 139:7-10)

> But God has revealed *them* to us through His Spirit. For the Spirit searches all things, yes, the deep things of God. For what man knows the things of a man except the spirit of the man which is in him?

Even so no one knows the things of God except the Spirit of God. (1 Corinthians 2:10-11)

While on this subject, we need to dispel the myth that the Holy Spirit is just a force. I have heard professing Christians – even charismatic or Pentecostal Christians, who emphasize the work of the Spirit – refer to the Holy Spirit as "it". The Holy Spirit is never referred to in the Bible as "it" – the Holy Spirit is always "Him". The Holy Spirit speaks personally. "As they ministered to the Lord and fasted, the Holy Spirit said, 'Now separate to Me Barnabas and Saul for the work to which I have called them.'" (Acts 13:2) An impersonal force does not speak, nor does it use the personal pronoun "I". This passage in Acts shows that the Holy Spirit is a person, not a force.

The Holy Spirit has a mind. Forces do not have minds. "And he who searches our hearts knows the mind of the Spirit, because the Spirit intercedes for the saints in accordance with God's will." (Romans 8:27). The Holy Spirit can also be grieved by our actions. "And do not **grieve** the Holy Spirit of God, by whom you were sealed for the day of redemption." (Ephesians 4:30) Forces cannot be grieved.

In summary, we have seen that the Holy Spirit is a person, who has emotions and personality. He has all the necessary divine attributes to be God, and is referred to as God.

One in three and three in one

We have now established that there is only one God. We have also established that there are three persons called God. Both these facts are true. It is from the combination of these facts that we infer the doctrine of the Trinity. Although critics are right in suggesting that the word Trinity does not appear in scripture, the word was actually made to describe an actual doctrine which is indeed found in the Bible. We could equally point out that the term Virgin Birth is not found in the Bible, but it is clearly taught.

Many theologians have admitted that the concept of the Trinity is difficult to get our heads around. Just because something is difficult, however, does not make it untrue. In fact, the very difficulty of the concept suggests to some of us that the doctrine is true, because it is unlikely that such a concept would be made up to try to explain God.

> Three in One and One in Three,
> Ruler of the earth and sea,
> hear us while we lift to thee
> holy chant and psalm[12].

We refer to the three persons of the Trinity as *persons* and not *people*. They are not three different and temporary entities – there is only one God. Yet there are distinctions between them. One common heresy, which we will examine later, is the concept of modalism, which suggests that the three persons are merely different manifestations of the one person. That is to say, when God is being Jesus, He is not being the Father. In contrast, the Bible lays down distinctions between the persons of the Trinity, while insisting that there is one God. All three persons are therefore of one substance. Yet the Father is not the Son or the Spirit, the Son is not the Father or the Spirit

---

[12] A hymn by **Gilbert Rorison (1821-1869),** this version taken from the Complete Mission Praise, 2000.

and the Spirit is not the Father or the Son. The Son is described as *begotten* (John 3:16). The Father and the Spirit are not. The Holy Spirit proceeds from the Father, but not vice versa (John 15:26).

> But when the Helper comes, whom I shall send to you from the Father, the Spirit of truth who proceeds from the Father, He will testify of Me. (John 15:26)

This verse also shows that the Holy Spirit is sent by the Son and the Father, and not vice versa[13]. Therefore, there appear to be differences among the persons of

---

[13] The fact that this verse says that the Holy Spirit is sent by the Son is the reason for Western Christians believing that the Holy Spirit proceeds from both the Father and the Son. Although the verse does not explicitly say that the Holy Spirit proceeds from the Son, such a relationship seems to be implied. Arguments over whether the Spirit proceeds from both the Father and the Son, or just from the Father, were at the heart of the schism between Western Christianity (i.e. the Roman Catholic Church) and Eastern Christianity (i.e. the various Orthodox churches) in AD 1054. The argument had gone on since AD 589, when the phrase "and from the Son" was added to the Nicene Creed, which had previously merely stated that the Holy Spirit proceeds from the Father. The Latin for the phrase "and from the Son" is *filioque*, so the controversy became known as the Filioque Clause controversy. For more discussion of this issue, see Grudem, W (1994), **Systematic Theology**, (Leicester: IVP), pp246-247

the Trinity. This does not suggest that the three persons are not all divine. The Son is subject[14] to the Father in His humanity, but is equal in His divinity. And all are one God – though it is not technically correct to say that they are all *part of* one God.

The language we use in describing the Trinity is critical. We refer to *persons* not people – *begotten* not created, and not born – *one God* not three parts. Again, it must be emphasized that the complexity of this teaching is part of the evidence of its truthfulness.

So, now that we have emphasized the teaching of the doctrine of the Trinity, we should look at some specific passages in the Bible, interpreting them in the light of Trinitarian teaching.

---

[14] It is quite difficult to find the right word to describe the relationship of the persons within the Trinity. 'Subject' may not be the correct word, but I hope readers will understand the point I am trying to get across. In my defence, I am using the same term here as used by Boice in Boice, JM, *Foundations of the Christian Faith*, (Leicester: IVP), p115

The Trinity in the New Testament

Matthew 28:18-19

And Jesus came and spoke to them, saying, 'All authority has been given to Me in heaven and on earth. Go therefore and make disciples of all the nations, baptizing them in the name of the Father and of the Son and of the Holy Spirit.'

There are some who assume that this is the only passage in which the Trinity appears. This is not the case, though these verses are a clear enunciation of the doctrine.

We can learn several things from this short passage.

Jesus has all authority in heaven and on earth. This suggests Jesus' omnipotence. If He has authority over all of this, then He is divine. And yet, the authority that He has is given to Him. If He has all authority, then He is supreme, but surely authority can only be given by someone who is equal or greater – the Father. If Jesus' possession of all authority implies His divinity, and the fact that He has been given the authority implies a distinction of persons between Him and the

Father, then these opening remarks are already beginning to give us an indication of the relationship of the first two persons of the Trinity. Then Jesus says "Go, therefore". The word *therefore* implies that the reason for going is given by the preceding phrase. The reason for going out into the world is because Jesus is divine and has authority, which He is exercising on behalf of the entire Godhead. Our job in going out is to make disciples and to baptize them. This chapter cannot give more information on the subject of baptism – though there is clearly a lot more to be said. However, we will simply note for now that the Trinity can also be seen at another baptism – the baptism of Jesus Himself, which we will analyze next. For now, let us look at the mode of baptism. Disciples are to be baptized in the name.... The word name is singular. They are not baptized into the names of the Father, Son and Holy Spirit. Disciples are baptized into a singular name. Once again, this implies that there is one God, in three persons. Then Jesus lists those persons – Father, Son and Holy Spirit. He has repeatedly emphasized that He is the Son, so this passage underlines the divinity of Jesus, in His own words, as well as underlining the Trinity itself.

Modalists will often refuse to use this baptism formula, baptizing only in the name of Jesus. They argue that this is because of Acts 19:4. For this reason, modalists are often referred to as "Jesus Name" or "Jesus Only" Christians. We will examine the interpretation of Acts 19:4 later in this chapter, when we look at anti-Trinitarian heresies, such as modalism.

Luke 3:21-22

> When all the people were baptized, it came to pass that Jesus also was baptized; and while He prayed, the heaven was opened. And the Holy Spirit descended in bodily form like a dove upon Him, and a voice came from heaven which said, 'You are My beloved Son; in You I am well pleased.'

It is significant that all three persons of the Trinity are present in this account. The account concerns the baptism of Jesus. Many articles have been written on the precise issues behind the occasion when Jesus was baptized. We know that the baptism practiced by John was a baptism of repentance[15], and it was for this reason that John himself expressed concerns about baptizing Jesus[16].

This passage is not only an affirmation of the Trinity, but also a clear refutation of modalism, as all three persons of the Trinity are present and in some form of communication with each other. The Holy Spirit proceeds from the Father. The Father verbally affirms His Son, and the Son is obedient to the Father. In view of the importance of the "name of the Father, the Son and the Holy Spirit" in the Great Commission above, it is especially appropriate that all three persons of the One God (Trinity) are manifest at the same time at the baptism of Jesus.

There seem to be so many heresies surrounding these events. One such heresy suggests that Jesus did not become the Christ and did not become divine until

---

[15] "And he (John) went into all the region around the Jordan, preaching a **baptism** of **repentance** for the remission of sins"(Luke 3:3)

[16] "And John *tried to* prevent Him, saying, 'I need to be baptized by You, and are You coming to me?' But Jesus answered and said to him, 'Permit *it to be so* now, for thus it is fitting for us to fulfill all righteousness.' Then he allowed Him." (Matthew 3:14-15)

His baptism. This heresy will be dealt with, in depth, in the chapter on the deity of Jesus. However, a couple of small comments on the deity of Christ are needed in this section, and are given below.

Acts 2:32-33

> This Jesus God has raised up, of which we are all witnesses. Therefore being exalted to the right hand of God, and having received from the Father the promise of the Holy Spirit, He poured out this which you now see and hear.

This passage is part of Peter's famous sermon at Pentecost. A similar formulation is seen in this passage, to the baptism of Jesus. Jesus is affirmed as divine by the Father – because only an equal can sit at the right hand of God. Therefore Jesus is God. Also, we see the Holy Spirit once again proceeding from the Father. There is rightly a lot of talk about the Holy Spirit in the events surrounding Pentecost, at what might be called the inauguration of the New Testament church. This passage additionally emphasizes the centrality of the whole Trinity to the birth of the church.

2 Corinthians 13:14

This beautiful short benediction is found in the epistles, and it emphasizes apostolic teaching.

> The grace of the Lord Jesus Christ, and the love of God, and the communion of the Holy Spirit *be* with you all. Amen.

This benediction denotes the work of all three persons of the Trinity in the salvation of a believer.

1 Peter 1:1-2

> Peter, an apostle of Jesus Christ,
>
> To the pilgrims of the Dispersion in Pontus, Galatia, Cappadocia, Asia, and Bithynia, elect according to the foreknowledge of God the Father, in sanctification of the Spirit, for obedience and sprinkling of the blood of Jesus Christ:
>
> Grace to you and peace be multiplied.

In a similar manner, the opening of Peters's first epistle emphasizes the work of all three persons in the lives of believers.

The Trinity in the Old Testament

Some might argue that the Trinity is a concept introduced in the New Testament. A Jewish person, therefore, might note that the concept couldn't be possible, until Christianity began, as they would maintain that the Trinity is a construct, in order to accommodate the deity of Jesus.

In the next chapter, we shall see how the Old Testament actually teaches the deity of Jesus. For now, let us confine ourselves to those passages that strongly imply the Trinity.

Isaiah 48:16-17

Come near to Me, hear this: I have not spoken in secret from the beginning; From the time that it was, I *was* there. And now the Lord GOD and His Spirit Have sent Me. Thus says the LORD, your Redeemer, The Holy One of Israel: " I am the LORD your God, Who teaches you to profit, Who leads you by the way you should go."

There appear to be three persons in this passage. One is the speaker, one is the Lord God and one is the

Spirit. The Lord God and the Spirit are both involved in sending the speaker.

Our first job in interpreting this remarkable passage is to work out who the speaker is. We are told in verse 17 – "Thus says the LORD, your Redeemer...". The speaker is therefore both LORD and Redeemer. We will come back to God being the Redeemer in a moment. First, we note that the word "LORD", as used in many English translations, is actually the so-called Tetragrammaton – the divine name of God, YHWH (often mistranslated as Jehovah). This is the same name as is given by God to Moses, when He appeared in the burning bush.

> And God said to Moses, "I AM WHO I AM." And He said, "Thus you shall say to the children of Israel, 'I AM has sent me to you.'" Moreover God said to Moses, "Thus you shall say to the children of Israel: 'The LORD God of your fathers, the God of Abraham, the God of Isaac, and the God of Jacob, has sent me to you.[17]

---

[17] Exodus 3:14-15

The Hebrew word for "I AM" is YHWH, and it is the same word which, elsewhere in most English translations, is translated LORD, with four capital letters. YHWH is identified as God. Yet, in Isaiah 48, the speaker, who we have identified as YHWH, is sent by God and His Spirit. The term "redeemer" implies someone who is buying back what is lost.

My maternal grandfather, having come from an upper middle-class merchant family, had developed a gambling habit. When he was out of work, in the 1920s, he would sometimes take an object from the house, such as a clock, to the local pawnbrokers, to get money to put on the horses. When my grandmother came home from her shift at the cotton mill, she would have to return to work to do an extra shift, to earn some more money. She could then take the extra money down to the pawnbrokers to redeem the item that her husband had taken. Redemption came at a price. If YHWH is described here as our redeemer, then this redemption was to come at a price. So the YHWH of Isaiah 48 refers to God and His Spirit as different persons, yet He is Himself identified as God. Yet we are repeatedly reminded us throughout the book of Isaiah that there is only one God.

> Before Me there was no God formed,
> And there will be none after Me. (Isaiah 43:10)

The only logical explanation is that the book of Isaiah is presenting God as One God, in three persons. This is, therefore, an Old Testament statement of the Trinity. We can say still more about the speaker in Isaiah 48.

> Listen to Me, O Jacob, And Israel, My called: I *am* He, I *am* the First, I *am* also the Last. Indeed My hand has laid the foundation of the earth, And My right hand has stretched out the heavens. (Isaiah 48:12-13)

Who is described in the Bible as "the First and the Last". It is clear that this language is used about God. Yet we read in Revelation 1:17-18

> I am the First and the Last. I am He who lives, and was dead, and behold, I am alive forevermore.

This language can only refer to Jesus, and, indeed, these passages at the beginning of Revelation are helpful in our understanding that Jesus is God. This agrees with Isaiah 48, where YHWH is God, yet is a different person from the one who sent Him, who is described as God, and we have also seen that YHWH is the redeemer – that He is to have to do something to redeem, which will clearly cost Him. In just 5 chapters time – Isaiah 53 – we find out what that redemption was to cost.

Genesis 1

Once we have established that the doctrine of the Trinity is taught, even in the Old Testament, we can see the teaching in the book of Genesis, and actually in the very first chapter. Genesis 1 does not *prove* the Trinity to us, but we can best understand it, once we have accepted that God is Trinity.

The first verse of the Bible is:

> In the beginning, God created the heavens and the earth.

The Hebrew word for God is *Elohim*. This is a plural word. The singular form would be *eloah*. Actually, the situation is more complex than this. Hebrew does not just have singular and plural forms. It actually has forms for singular, dual and plural, where plural must mean at least three. *Elohim* is a plural form, so must mean at least three. However, the verb for created (*bara*) is in singular form. So we have a triply plural noun with a singular verb. This construction agrees well with the concept of the Trinity. Knowing what we now do, from elsewhere in scripture, we quickly see all three persons of the Trinity active in the creation. We have God Himself, and we have the Spirit of God. Slightly less obvious is that we have the Word of God – as in "God said 'Let there be light...'" The Hebrew for "to say" is *mr*. From this root is derived the rabbinical word *memra*, which means "Word" – however, it is not "word" in the sense of a simple word – that would be *davar*. *Memra* is Word with a capital W.

This latter point is further underlined by looking at the Jewish Targums. A targum is, in a sense, a paraphrase of the Old Testament. It is a little more complicated than that. A particular group of rabbis would approve a targum, as a correct representation of what the Bible actually says at the point of scripture under interpretation, as they translated it from Hebrew into Aramaic. There is, therefore, a level of authority associated with a targum – albeit a level of human intellectual authority. Many of the targums use the word *memra* in conjunction with passages that speak about God in His dealing with people. For example, look at the targum interpretations below:

> The Word [*memra*] of the Lord created man. (Genesis 1:27)

> And Abraham believed in the Word of the Lord. (Genesis 15:6)

> Israel will be saved by the Word of the Lord. (Isaiah 45:17)[18]

This rabbinical tradition of referring to God, in passages that we consider to be referring to the

---

[18] Hughes, M. (2008), **Jewish Reflections on the Nature of God: The Logos/Memra of the Lord**, < http://www.foundationsmin.org/studies/memra.htm >, (retrieved 12th November 2009)

Second Person of the Trinity, would have been well known in New Testament times. So, the opening sentences of John's Gospel would have been relating a style already known to many readers. What was new in John's writing was not his use of the concept of the Word (*Logos* in Greek), because this is the same concept as the rabbinical concept of *memra*. What is new is John's clear application of the concept of Logos/Memra to Jesus.

Which brings us back to Genesis 1. We have seen above that one targum represents Genesis 1:27 as saying that man was created by the Word of the Lord. Add to this a remarkable passage from the Targum Neofiti, dated about 200BC:

> In the beginning, by the firstborn, God created the heavens and the earth. (Genesis 1:1)[19]

The Targum Neofiti uses the concept of *firstborn* to mean preeminent, rather than to imply that there was

---

[19] Quoted by Driscoll, M. And Breshears, G., in their forthcoming book, **Doctrine: What Christians Should Believe**, (Crossway: 2010) – I found an extract from this book on Gerry Breshear's blog, < http://breshears.net/?page_id=482 >, retrieved 12th November 2009.

a beginning. This understanding of the term *firstborn* can be seen elsewhere in scripture, using standard translations. For example, in Jeremiah, God describes Ephraim as His firstborn.

> For I am a Father to Israel, And Ephraim is My firstborn. (Jeremiah 31:9).

This is because of Ephraim's pre-eminence over Manasseh, because, in chronological terms, it was Manasseh who was born before his brother Ephraim.

> Joseph called the name of the firstborn Manasseh. (Genesis 41:51)

So the use of the term *firstborn* in the Targum Neofiti's rendition of Genesis 1:1 implies that the Word (*memra*) of God was there at the beginning, and responsible for creation – exactly as John's Gospel puts it! Therefore, we get all three persons of the Trinity demonstrated in the first chapter of the Bible.

Anti-Trinitarian Heresies and Rejections of the Trinity

We have to admit that the doctrine of the Trinity is not an easy subject. We have noted, however, that the doctrine's very complexity is one of the arguments for its authenticity – an artificial religion would not have made such a doctrine up.

Because of the difficulties that people have with the doctrine, there has been a tendency of late for pastors not to preach on the subject. There has tended to be an assumption that, because a church has the doctrine in its statement of faith, everyone in the church believes it. The truth is that many church members will believe that they believe the doctrine – but in practice will often have ideas that are broadly influenced by the errors below.

Polytheism

The first collection of errors will be those who acknowledge at least a form of deity for the Son and Holy Spirit, but will say that these are really the evidence for a multiplicity of gods. One 'Christian' grouping that teaches this line of thinking is the

Church of Jesus Christ of Latter Day Saints, commonly known as the Mormons. There is not the space in this current study to make a detailed criticism of Mormonism, and others have tackled this better than I could[20]. Suffice it to say that Mormonism is both polytheistic and evolutionary in character, believing that God and Jesus have developed into the roles which they now have, and that we can do likewise. One of the Mormon Church's presidents once put it this way:

> As man is, God once was; As God is, man may become.[21]

However, this paragraph is not specifically a criticism of Mormonism alone. Some 'Christian' leaders have made similar errors. For example, Kenneth Copeland has said:

> You don't have a God in you – you are one.[22]

---

[20] See, for example, Ankerberg, J. & Weldon, J. (2003), **Fast Facts on Mormonism**, (Harvest House Publishers)

[21] Lorenzo Snow, Fifth LDS President, 1840.

[22] Copeland, K. (1987) *The Force of Love* (audio tape), Kenneth Copeland Ministries, Fort Worth, Texas, #02-0028

I know that people worry about such comments, that they might be taken out of context. Copeland was referring to a sort of divinity of human beings. He was not claiming that we are God – but that our mode of creation makes us gods. Just to rule out the error of quoting out of context, Copeland went on to say in the same message:

> [Adam] was not subordinate to God....What he said, went. What he did, counted. [And when he] bowed his knee to Satan and put Satan up above him, then there wasn't anything God could do about it, because a *god* had placed [Satan] there.[23]

Joyce Meyer has made similar claims. Once again, it must be emphasized that she is not claiming that we are God - "capital G" is how she qualifies it – but that we are little gods[24]. I have to say I am not an over-enthusiastic critic of Joyce Meyer, and I suspect that, if she were questioned specifically on this issue, that she would backtrack, but it is indicative of the sort of

---

[23] *ibid*

[24] Regrettably, I have been unable to find a transcript for this talk. However, I accessed the audio of the talk from YouTube on 15th November 2009.

loose and sloppy thinking that allows us to think we are somehow similar to God, when scripture reminds us that "God is not a man..."[25]

The teaching that we, angels, or any other being are in any way gods is dangerous, and is a denial of the teaching of the Trinity.

Tritheism

The three persons of the Trinity are sometimes held, by certain groups, to be so distinct, that they actually constitute three gods. Very few groups throughout history have explicitly stated this belief. But the belief is there, among those who have an inadequate doctrine of the Trinity. However, the belief is usually more of an accusation than a belief. It is an accusation leveled against Christians by monotheistic faiths, such as Islam or Jehovah's Witnesses. It is usually a deliberate misunderstanding of the Trinity, and a failure to acknowledge the arguments laid out in the earlier section, headed "There is only one God".

---

[25] Numbers 23:19

It has to be acknowledged that there are those within supposedly Trinitarian churches who have emphasized such a distinction between the persons of the Trinity that they have become tritheists in all but name. An example of such 'popular', but mistaken, tritheist theology would be the version of the Trinity as portrayed in the popular fictional novel, *The Shack*. The problems with that book will be discussed later.

In responding to accusations of tritheism, it is necessary to emphasize the Bible's teaching that there is only one God.

Unitarianism

Unitarianism often seems to be defined by negatives – i.e. what they don't believe. They do not believe in the Trinity, the deity of Jesus, the inerrancy or authority of scripture, personhood of the Holy Spirit, eternal punishment or vicarious atonement of Jesus. Unitarianism has had some notable followers. The ideas of Arius were essentially Unitarian[26], as were

---

[26] **Arius**. (2009). In *Encyclopædia Britannica*. Retrieved November 16, 2009, from Encyclopædia Britannica Online: http://www.britannica.com/EBchecked/topic/34795/Arius

those of Michael Servetus[27], who was executed for heresy by the Calvinists in Geneva. Extreme liberalism and universalism is also at the heart of much Unitarianism. The website of The General Assembly of Unitarian and Free Christian Churches (Great Britain) states that:

> Unitarianism is an open-minded and individualistic approach to faith that gives scope for a very wide range of beliefs and doubts.
>
> Religious freedom for each individual is at the heart of Unitarianism. Everyone has the right to search for meaning in life and reach their own conclusions.
>
> Unitarians see diversity and pluralism as valuable rather than threatening. They want faith to be broad, inclusive, and tolerant. Unitarianism can therefore include people who are Christian, Jewish, Buddhist, Pagan and Atheist.[28]

[27] **Michael Servetus**. (2009). In *Encyclopædia Britannica*. Retrieved November 16, 2009, from Encyclopædia Britannica Online: http://www.britannica.com/EBchecked/topic/535958/Michael-Servetus

[28] **Are you a Unitarian?**, < http://www.unitarian.org.uk/intro/believe1.shtml >, retrieved 16th November 2009

Such inclusiveness, added to the unbiblical understanding of the nature of God and of Jesus, means that Unitarians cannot be described as biblical Christians.

There are other groups which take a broadly Unitarian view, including Jehovah's Witnesses and Christadelphians. People of Unitarian beliefs can also be found among many of the mixed denominations, including such groups as the Methodist Church and the Church of England.

Modalism

There are a number of religious groups that take what is known as a Oneness position. Oneness is also sometimes referred to as *Jesus Name*, or *modalism*, for reasons that will become clear shortly. Such groups are also known as Sabellianist, after Sabellius, a third century theologian, who formulated ideas similar to modern Oneness theology.

Outwardly, modalists appear orthodox. They claim to belief the Bible to be inerrant, and they refer to the unsaved as sinners in need of repentance. However, they differ considerably from orthodoxy on the subject of the Trinity. Their view is that "Father", "Son" and "Holy Spirit" are three different *modes* of operation of the One God. A pastor of a oneness denomination in Ireland described Jesus to me as "simply God manifest in the flesh". Use of language is so important in such matters. Trinitarian Christians would also describe Jesus as "God manifest in the flesh", but the difference is that modalists are denying the personhood of Jesus, and maintaining that God is represented in different temporary modes, not persons.

As part of our evidence for the Trinity above, I used the verse in Matthew 28:19, where we are told to "Go therefore and make disciples of all the nations, baptizing them in the name of the Father and of the Son and of the Holy Spirit". We noted that the word *name* is singular. Modalists maintain that the "name of the Father and of the Son and of the Holy Spirit" is indeed singular, and Jesus is that name. As evidence for this position, modalists offer such verses as Acts 19:5: "they were baptized in the name of the Lord

Jesus". Therefore, they baptize their believers only in the name of Jesus, which is one of the reasons why they are referred to as *Jesus Name* Christians. There are a number of refutations to this position. Firstly, the phrase "in the name of" is used throughout Matthew's Gospel to refer to the identity of the person concerned, not to introduce a different name. Secondly, the early church did not appear to have a formula for what should be said during baptism, and thirdly, at least one baptism "in Jesus name" only is seen to be inadequate:

> Now when the apostles who were at Jerusalem heard that Samaria had received the word of God, they sent Peter and John to them, who, when they had come down, prayed for them that they might receive the Holy Spirit. For as yet He had fallen upon none of them. They had only been baptized in the name of the Lord Jesus. Then they laid hands on them, and they received the Holy Spirit. (Acts 8:14-17)

Modalism is found in a number of denominations and church groupings, such as the Churches of God in Ireland, and the United Pentecostal Church and New

Apostolic Church (the latter not to be confused with the Apostolic Church (UK), which is a classical Trinitarian Pentecostal denomination). However, modalism can also be found among groups that otherwise appear orthodox.

An example of the above is the accusation made against the TV preacher, TD Jakes. Jakes has been accused of making statements which are similar to modalism[29]. It has to be stated in fairness that Jakes has denied the accusation[30]. Yet in Jakes's response, he doesn't seem to be able to come out and endorse the doctrine of the Trinity. His fairly vague statements include the following:

> We have one God, but He is Father in creation, Son in redemption, and Holy Spirit in regeneration.[31]

[29] LeBlanc, D., **Theology: Apologetics Journal Criticizes Jakes**, Christianity Today, February 7th 2000, < http://www.christianitytoday.com/ct/2000/february7/5.58.html >, retrieved November 16th 2009

[30] Jakes, TD, **My Views on the Godhead**, Christianity Today, February 21st 2000, < http://www.christianitytoday.com/ct/2000/februaryweb-only/13.0b.html >

[31] *Living by The Word*, radio interview with T. D. Jakes, KKLA 99.5, Los Angeles, 23 and 30 August 1998, quoted in Buckner, J.L., **Concerns about the Teachings of TD Jakes**, Christian Research Journal, Vol. 22 no. 2 (1999)

While it is feasible that a Trinitarian might have used such language, it has to be said that Jakes's comment is identical to the claims of modalism. At the very least, this is a poor use of language. At worst, it shows that there are those who seem to be within mainstream evangelism or pentecostalism who hold views consistent with modalism.

A variant of modalism – and a corollary of it – is the doctrine known as patripassionism. In this doctrine, it was the Father who became flesh and therefore who died physically on the cross. The doctrine supposes that Jesus and the Father are one, claiming that this was what Jesus Himself said.

I and *My* Father are one. (John 10:30)

However, the context makes clear that Jesus was not claiming to be the same *person* as the Father – in just the previous verse, He had talked about the Father giving believers to Him (Jesus). Jesus was claiming, not the same personhood, but the same substance.

The Trinity in Creation

We have seen earlier that the Trinity is implied in Genesis 1. Having established that the Bible teaches the doctrine of the Trinity, rather than any of the alternative positions, we can now go on to see the Trinity reflected in various aspects of nature.

One famous analogy of the Trinity is that of the three states of matter. Under normal conditions, most compounds can exist in one of three phases – solid, liquid and gas[32]. Molecules of H_2O, for example, can exist as ice, water and steam. Indeed, there is a special temperature and pressure, known as the Triple Point, where all three phases coexist in dynamic equilibrium. In the case of water, the Triple Point is a temperature of 273.16 kelvins and a pressure of 611.2 pascals[33]. This concept has frequently been used as an analogy for the Trinity, but it should not be pushed too far. Normally,

---

[32] The so-called fourth state of matter – plasma – does not really count in this analogy, because it involves a complete change in atomic structure, whereas the traditional three states only involve changes in inter-molecular attractions.

[33] 0°C, the freezing point of water, is 273.15K, so the triple point is at 0.01°C. Standard atmospheric pressure is 101 325 Pa, so the Triple Point is at just over half of 1% of atmospheric pressure.

the three phases do not exist at the same time – so the concept could be used as an analogy by the modalists! If the analogy is used of the Triple point, then it is slightly better, but it is only an analogy. The purpose of mentioning the three phases here is not actually to make an analogy. The existence of Trinity-like analogies in creation does not prove the Trinity. Rather it is the other way around. Given that the Trinity is a fact, we would expect to see Trinitarian analogues in creation. It is the presupposition of the Trinity that helps us interpret the creation, not the other way around.

Having seen that there is a Trinitarian analogue in matter, we can also see Trinitarian analogues in space and time. Time exists as past, present and future. Space exists in three dimensions – length, width and height. Taken together, matter, time and space are the three domains of the universe. So these domains themselves form a sort-of trinity, while each domain is itself a sort-of trinity. Therefore we have a trinity of trinities. Once again, we must emphasize that these analogies of the Trinity are not proofs for the Trinity, nor are they fully satisfactory as analogies. We are merely noting that such analogies are likely to exist, given that the universe was created by God the Trinity.

Following these analogies, we start to see other analogies thick and fast. What, for example, is the most rigid possible shape? It is, of course, the triangle, and its rigidity is put to use in structures, such as this crane.

Understanding and Believing the Trinity

So why did I start this chapter in such an odd way? I was trying to make a point – that a great many people in ordinary churches do not understand the doctrine of the Trinity as they ought. Don't get me wrong – it is such a deep, big and complex doctrine, that I don't expect many people to fathom its depths. However, most Christians seem not to have taken the time to get their ideas right on the Trinity.

The argument too often is that we shouldn't divide over secondary issues. The problem is that the Trinity is simply not a secondary issue – it is a primary issue. The Athanasian Creed quoted above makes clear that belief in the Trinity is a sign that you are saved – it is not possible to be saved while disbelieving this doctrine, because, if you do disbelieve the Trinity, you have not recognized the essential nature of God.

Unitarian, or modalist views of God simply are inadequate.

Beloved, let us love one another, for love is of God; and everyone who loves is born of God and knows God. He who does not love does not know God, for God is love. In this the love of God was manifested toward us, that God has sent His only begotten Son into the world, that we might live through Him. (1 John 4:7-9)

This is the passage where we get the famous phrase, "God is love". But a monotheistic view of God does not allow for a God, whose very nature is love. Let me explain what I mean. One children's book that I once read started with by saying that God was lonely, so He decided to make a world. What a cute idea! But, you see, God was never lonely. There was an eternal loving relationship between the Father, the Son and the Holy Spirit from eternity past. God didn't need us to fill some emptiness within Him – He had all the community and love He needed. Therefore He made us for His own good pleasure, and gave us the ability to love, because we are in His image. The Unitarians do not have an eternal concept of God's love – nor do the Christadelphians or the Muslims or the Modalists. It is only the orthodox evangelical Christians who can understand that God is love, because He has always been love and always shall be.

So the acceptance of the doctrine of the Trinity has very practical and devotional outcomes for those who accept it. Yet the doctrine seems to be rarely taught from pulpits. This means that it is likely that many Christians will have a view of the Trinity formulated only on the back of such fiction as "The Shack" by W. Paul Young.

This is not the space for a detailed review of The Shack. You will find an excellent and thorough review at the Discerning Reader website[34]. For now, let's just pick out three errors. The main character, Mack, meets the Trinity in the eponymous shack. All three persons of the Trinity are present, and refer to each other separately, in a manner which is reminiscent of tritheism. The Father is actually represented by a middle-aged black woman, called Papa. This would appear to be a contradiction of the second

---

[34] < http://www.challies.com/sites/all/files/files/The_Shack.pdf >

commandment. In one scene, Mack notices that Papa has marks on his wrists and feet. This is patripassionism. At other points, there are descriptions and events that appear to point to modalism. In short, The Shack is not a book to help the reader understand the Trinity – it is a confused book, which will sew even more confusion.

One problem in our current society is that we do always need to ask why. Asking why can be good – but sometimes, we simply need to accept some teaching at face value. The Trinity is one such teaching. It is not difficult to accept, even if it is difficult to comprehend.

1. There is one God.

2. God exists in three persons – Father, Son and Holy Spirit, but is just one God.

3. The Father is God, the Son is God and the Holy Spirit is God. There is just one God.

4. The Father is not the Spirit nor the Son – the Son is not the Father nor the Spirit, and the

Spirit is not the Father nor the Son. They are each of three persons, yet one God.

5. There is just one God in three persons.

Holy, holy, holy! Lord God Almighty!
Early in the morning our song shall rise to thee.
Holy, holy, holy! Merciful and mighty,
God in three persons, blessed Trinity!

Genesis and the Deity of Christ

Who was this Jesus, anyway? Everyone seems to have their own view of who He was, or what He was like. It seems to be open season. Anyone can decide what they think He is like. Do you remember the Depeche Mode song?

> Reach out and touch faith
> Your own Personal Jesus
> Someone to hear your prayers
> Someone who cares
> Your own Personal Jesus
> Someone to hear your prayers
> Someone who's there[1]

The songwriter Martin Gore says that the song was influenced by Priscilla Presley's book, *Elvis and Me.*

> It's a song about being a Jesus for somebody else, someone to give you hope and care. It's about how Elvis was her man and her mentor and how often that happens in love relationships; how

---

[1] Gore, ML, *Personal Jesus*, recorded by Depeche Mode, August 29, 1989

everybody's heart is like a god in some way. We play these god-like parts for people but no one is perfect, and that's not a very balanced view of someone is it?[2]

Regardless of whether or not the song or book are on this theme, the comment and the lyrics are referring to how we can make up our own religion. Yet we are not just talking about having a personal god – we are talking about a personal Jesus. The name Jesus means "The LORD saves". People are looking for a savior – but it has to be a savior on our own terms. We want to be saved from the things that we find difficult, so that we can get on and live our lives.

That means we install a Jesus in our lives, who is not the same as the Jesus of the Bible. It is the Bible which describes the Son of God to us. If our description of Jesus differs from that of the Bible, then it is not the real Jesus that we are talking about – we are talking about a false Messiah.

[2] Spin vol 6 number 4, July 1990, < http://www.tuug.utu.fi/~jaakko/dm/spinmode.html >

This ought to be a matter that concerns us deeply. If people are worshipping a false Messiah, and not the real Jesus, then they are not saved. Yet it is often our desire to be inclusive. Surely if someone confesses the name of Jesus, then they must be Christians, mustn't they?

> If you confess with your mouth the Lord Jesus and believe in your heart that God has raised Him from the dead, you will be saved. (Romans 10:9)

The problem inherent in the misquotation of Romans 10:9 is that one often fails to define what is meant by "believe in your heart". It is not just a matter of giving a mental assent to the fact of the resurrection. Indeed, just a few verses earlier, this has been couched in terms of submission.

> For they being ignorant of God's righteousness, and seeking to establish their own righteousness, have not submitted to the righteousness of God. (Romans 10:3)

So a mere mental assent to the name Jesus would not appear to be sufficient. It is important to understand that knowing the character of Jesus from the Bible is important, as well as simply acknowledging His name.

To explain this further, imagine someone saying that they knew the Queen. Then imagine that they described her as a very tall lady, with long, flowing, blond hair. "That's not the Queen", you would protest. "Yes it is!" they reply. "She was introduced to me as the Queen".

If you have been introduced to the wrong Jesus, it makes no difference if you protest that others know the same Jesus. What really matters is if you know the right Jesus.

Some believe Jesus was just a man and not divine

Some religious groups, and many individuals, believe that Jesus was a good man, but was not God. This is a fairly common position to take. In fact, the opinion that Jesus was a good man can be found outside Christianity. Consider these quotes below:

In reality there has been only one Christian, and he died on the Cross. (Nietzsche)[3]

A man who was completely innocent, offered himself as a sacrifice for the good of others, including his enemies, and became the ransom of the world. It was a perfect act. (Mahatma Gandhi)[4]

Jesus was the first socialist, the first to seek a better life for mankind. (Mikhail Gorbachev)[5]

2,000 years ago one man got nailed to a tree for saying how great it would be if everyone was nice to each other for a change. (Douglas Adams)[6]

These quotes are all "in favor" of Jesus, but do not attribute him with divine qualities. Far from it. Gandhi, for example, goes further.

---

[3] Nietzsche, quoted in Hollingdale, R.J. (2001), *Nietzshe: The Man and his Philosophy*, (Cambridge: Cambridge University Press), p208

[4] Quoted in Gandhi, R. (2008), *Gandhi: the man, his people, and the empire*, (Berkely, CA: University of California Press), p538

[5] Quoted in Daily Telegraph (16 June 1992)

[6] Adams, D. *The Hitchhiker's Guide to the Galaxy*, (Pan books)

> I cannot say that Jesus was uniquely divine. He was
> as much God as Krishna, or Rama, or Mohammed,
> or Zoroaster. (Gandhi)[7]

I have not done an opinion poll to find out what the majority view in the UK is about Jesus, but I would suspect that it might be along those lines - an opinion that Jesus was good, but not unique, blessed but not divine. As we will see, such a view is not compatible with scripture, nor is it actually logical. But few people allow logic to get in the way of a good argument.

It has to be said that some of the problem that the wider public has in recognizing Jesus as God may stem from the outpourings of so-called Christian clergy. Prominent among these was David Jenkins, who was Bishop of Durham in the Church of England from 1984 to 1994. He cast doubt on an actual physical resurrection of Jesus, believing it to have been just spiritual. He also claimed that people who did not

---

[7] I cannot find a book reference for this quote, though it must exist. I found it quoted at < http://www.finestquotes.com/select_quote_category-Jesus-page-0.htm >

believe that Jesus was and is God could still call themselves Christians.[8]

Jenkins made a name for himself by his unorthodox beliefs. Yet one of his successors has made an equally recognizable name for himself, by espousing what he calls evangelical doctrine - that is Dr NT Wright. In a video short filmed for the BioLogos Foundation, Wright discusses the humanity and divinity of Jesus, rightly emphasizing both. However, he strays from orthodoxy when he insists that the humanity of Jesus means that he could have had doubts about his own divinity.

> One thing that I meet constantly and have done for many years is the idea that because Jesus was divine... He couldn't have had any questions in his mind.... He couldn't actually have meant it when he said "maybe there's another way" in Gethsemene.[9]

[8]   <   http://www.independent.co.uk/opinion/profile-the-one-true-bishop-of-durham-dr-david-jenkins-retiring-scourge-of-sacred-cows-1392030.html >

[9] *Understanding the humanity of Jesus*, NT Wright and Peter Enns, BioLogos Foundation,   <   http://biologos.org/blog/understanding-the-humanity-of-

This sort of criticism of orthodoxy is more difficult to tackle than the outright rejectionism represented by Jenkins and his ilk. Wright emphasizes the humanity and the deity of Jesus - an opinion on which I agree with Wright, and to which we will return later in this chapter. Yet Wright's view of Jesus' humanity actually undermines Jesus' divinity. He describes Jesus as having questions about Himself - yet even in childhood, we see Jesus fully knowledgeable about His ministry - asking His parents "Did you not know that I must be about My Father's business?" (Luke 2:49). Wright suggests that Jesus had pondered "maybe there is another way", when He was in Gethsemene. That is a clear misunderstanding of what was actually happening in that Garden. Jesus did not actually say that. What Jesus actually said was "Father, if it is Your will, take this cup away from Me; nevertheless not My will, but Yours, be done." (Luke 22:42) Does this really mean that Jesus wanted to find "another way"? Hardly! Note carefully this well-known exchange below.

jesus/ >

> From that time Jesus began to show to His
> disciples that He must go to Jerusalem, and suffer
> many things from the elders and chief priests and
> scribes, and be killed, and be raised the third day.
> Then Peter took Him aside and began to rebuke
> Him, saying, "Far be it from You, Lord; this shall
> not happen to You!" But He turned and said to
> Peter, "Get behind Me, Satan! You are an offense
> to Me, for you are not mindful of the things of God,
> but the things of men." (Matthew 16:21-23)

Peter had only just been commended for declaring
that Jesus was the Christ, yet now Jesus describes him
as "Satan" and "an offense to Me". What had Peter
done to earn his Lord's ire? He had rebuked Jesus for
saying that He would be killed and rise again on the
third day. Jesus was not, even in His humanity, looking
to avoid his crucifixion. John Macarthur puts it like this.

> This does not imply that there was any conflict
> between the will of the Father and the will of the
> Son. It was a perfectly normal expression of His
> humanity that He shrank from the cup of divine
> wrath. But even though the cup was abhorrent to

Him, He willingly took it, because it was the will of the Father.[10]

Full blown unitarianism, with a small u, is found not only in churches that use the word Unitarian in their name, but also in some mainstream denominations. After all, I have observed around the UK that many Unitarian congregations have developed from Presbyterian congregations. For example, the famous Cross Street Chapel in Manchester started in 1662 as a congregation of Dissenters and Nonconformists excluded from Anglican worship. Indeed, the leader and founder of the original congregation was Henry Newcome, who had been made a Preacher at the Collegiate Church (which is now Manchester Cathedral) in 1657, but had been ordained as a Presbyterian. Newcome was a Trinitarian, but the church had been led into unitarianism by the middle of the 18th Century.[11]

---

[10] Macarthur, J., *The Macarthur Study Bible*, notes on Luke 22:42, (Thomas Nelson (NKJV): Nashville, Tennessee), p1561

[11] Head, G. *A Brief History of Cross Street Chapel*, < http://cross-street-chapel.org.uk/history >, accessed 8th September 2010.

Sometimes, the actual status of Jesus in unitarianism becomes somewhat symbolic. For example, the General Assembly of Unitarian and Free Christian Churches in the UK publish a number of explanatory leaflets. The following quote is taken from their publication Unitarian Views of Jesus - An Introduction.[12]

> I would say it is entirely possible to acknowledge the divinity of Jesus AND be a Unitarian. When I look at Jesus I am not, in fact, seeing God. Instead I am seeing a reflection of God – perhaps a perfect reflection – and in this sense I see Jesus as divine. What I deny is the DEITY of Jesus. I don't believe Jesus is God. This is why, among other reasons, I'm a Unitarian.

So often we find that analyzing unbiblical doctrines is like nailing jelly to the ceiling. The writer of this leaflet is trying to make a distinction between divinity and deity. The distinction is disingenuous. In this chapter, when I have been using the word divinity, I have made no such distinction, and the distinction is

---

[12] < www.unitarian.org.uk >, accessed 8th September 2010

unjustified either biblically or by dictionary definition.[13] However, the leaflet continues with the writer adding a further distinction - maintaining that there is a distinction between Jesus and Christ.

> In Jesus I see the Christ, the anointed, the chosen. When I say that I mean that I draw a distinction between the human Jesus and the Christ. How do I do this? Well, by saying that Jesus is the man and Christ is who he was called to be. Jesus is the human, Christ is the divine calling and promise that worked within him – and in Jesus these two things, for me, seem inseparable. In Jesus I see someone who so fully opened himself to his calling that I cannot see where the human ends and the Christ (the calling, the anointing) starts - yet he remained fully human. I see him as a human chosen to reveal God.

The writer is separating the concept of Jesus being the person from Christ being the office. Yet, biblically, there are no grounds for this separation. The idea of

---

[13] The Cambridge Dictionary, for example, defines 'Divine' as 'connected with a god, or like a god'.

such separation of person and office, however, is very old, and dates back to Arianism.

Arians, who follow the teachings of Arius, a Bishop of Alexandria who died in AD 336, make much of John's description of Jesus as "the only begotten Son" of God - notably in John 1:14; 3:16; 1 John 4:9. They argue that if Jesus were begotten, then He could not be eternal, as He must have been brought into existence by the Father. Arius's views were condemned by the Council of Nicea in AD 325. For this reason, the Nicene Creed's statement about Jesus is very tight and very firm.

> And [we believe] in one Lord Jesus Christ, the only-begotten Son of God, begotten of His Father before all worlds, God of God, Light of Light, very God of very God, begotten, not made, being of one substance with the Father.[14]

The creed uses the phrase "before all worlds" - often correctly interpreted as "before all ages". This term was added to the creed at the Council of

---

[14] Quoted in Ross, A., *The Son of God, Begotten not Made*, < http://bible.org/seriespage/son-god-begotten-not-made >, accessed 8th September 2010

Constantinople in AD 381, to make it even more watertight on this issue. Thus, we see that the word "begotten" does not imply that Jesus was "created" in some way by the Father. Rather, it simply illustrates the hierarchy in the Trinity and also underlines the eternal love that exists within the Godhead.

It is, moreover, Arianism that suggests that Christ took on divine nature. Arians refer to the concept of the *Logos*, which is the Greek word for 'word', and is used in John's Gospel - "In the beginning was the Word..." (John 1:1). Arians suggest that the *Logos* always existed, but that Jesus was conceived and became the *Logos* only at conception. Others, for example Christadelphians, believe that Jesus became "adopted" as the Son of God at His baptism. These ideas, known as *adoptionism*, are also not found in scripture. Biblical Christians would contend that Jesus' baptism is, in fact, a proof and verification of God as Trinity.

In contemporary evangelical churches, it is my contention that a concentration on the humanity of Jesus, in the sense of trying to make him "relevant", has sometimes been done at the expense of reverence for His divinity. Therefore, although it is not actually unitarianism that has gripped evangelicalism, it appears to be almost a tendency towards unitarianism. It can be appreciated that it can sometimes be difficult to get the balance of our utterances right - especially as there is the possibility of unbalance in the opposite direction, as outlined below. But just because this balance can be difficult does not mean that it should not be attempted.

Some believe Jesus was just divine and not human

This belief is perhaps stranger and rarer than the above, but it still exists, and it is an aberration that dates back to shortly after New Testament times, and is known as *docetism*, from the Greek δοκέω "to seem". The idea was that Jesus only *seemed* human, but could not in fact have a human body. Docetic views were common among gnostics, who tended to believe that matter is evil. Grudem reports on docetism in his *Systematic Theology* and ends this footnote with a severe warning.

Behind docetism is an assumption that the material creation is inherently evil, and therefore the Son of God could not have been united to a true human nature. No prominent church leader ever advocated docetism, but it was a troublesome heresy that had various supporters in the first four centuries of the church. Modern evangelicals who neglect to teach on the full humanity of Christ can unwittingly support docetic tendencies in their hearers.[15]

What Grudem seems to be saying is that sometimes we evangelicals can rightly be concerned to emphasize the divinity of Jesus. However, in so doing, we sometimes make this emphasis at the expense of Jesus' humanity, and therefore produce a tendency to lean towards docetism. But this is not the Jesus of the Bible. We are assured in scripture that Jesus was completely human. That is how He is able to understand us. Indeed, the Bible assures us not only that Jesus **was** completely human, but He **is** completely human.

---

[15] See Grudem, W. (1994), *Systematic Theology*, (Leicester: IVP), p540

> For we do not have a High Priest who cannot sympathize with our weaknesses, but was in all points tempted as we are, yet without sin. (Hebrews 4:15)

I agree with Grudem's concern. Not only that, but I would add that the tendency amongst evangelicals towards docetism actually pushes others - in an attempt to balance - towards the previous error of Unitarianism.

The Hypostatic Union

This discussion of biblical errors brings us to a consideration of the positive position, which is called the *Hypostatic Union*. In my view, this doctrine is as important as the doctrine of the Trinity. Like that other primary doctrine, the doctrine has a non-biblical name to describe a thoroughly biblical doctrine. In brief, the concept of the Hypostatic Union, is that Jesus Christ had/has two *natures* (human and divine) but is one *person*. In chapter 1, we commented that the Athanasian Creed has two great themes - the first is the Trinity, and the second is the Hypostatic

Union. For that reason, it might be of use to repeat the second section of the Creed, as quoted on page 17.

> Furthermore, it is necessary to everlasting salvation that he also believe rightly the Incarnation of our Lord Jesus Christ. For the right faith is, that we believe and confess, that our Lord Jesus Christ, the Son of God, is God and man; God, of the substance of the Father, begotten before the worlds; and man of the substance of his mother, born in the world; perfect God and perfect man, of a rational soul and human flesh subsisting. Equal to the Father, as touching His godhead; and inferior to the Father, as touching His manhood; who, although He is God and man, yet he is not two, but one Christ; one, not by conversion of the godhead into flesh but by taking of the manhood into God; one altogether; not by confusion of substance, but by unity of person. For as the rational soul and flesh is one man, so God and man is one Christ; who suffered for our salvation, descended into hell, rose again the third day from the dead. He ascended into heaven, He sits at the right hand of the Father, God Almighty, from

> whence He will come to judge the quick and the dead. At His coming all men will rise again with their bodies and shall give account for their own works. And they that have done good shall go into life everlasting; and they that have done evil into everlasting fire.

Athanasius thought that these issues were of primary importance. Indeed, he thought that without belief in these issues, one could not be saved.

> This is the catholic faith, which except a man believe faithfully, he cannot be saved.

Let's analyze Athanasius' excellent precepts a line at a time.

> For the right faith is, that we believe and confess...

This is the *right faith*. It is necessary to believe it, but also to confess that we believe it.

> ...that our Lord Jesus Christ, the Son of God

Jesus is both Lord and Christ, as Peter declares in Acts 2. He is the Son of God - with all the attributes that go with that phrase; for instance, see Psalm 2.

...is God and man;

This is the nub of the issue. Jesus is both God **and** man. Athanasius will now expand on this issue, but he wants to start by emphasizing this important truth of the two natures. Yet, if he stopped here, there could still have been confusion. When we say that Jesus is both God and man, what actually is He? Is He 50% God and 50% man? Is He man who became God? Or is He God who became man? Athanasius does not suggest any of those, as we shall see.

> God, of the substance of the Father, begotten before the worlds...

Arianism, mentioned above, suggested that Jesus was of *like* substance to the Father. The Greek word for this is *homoiousios*. Athanasius maintained that Jesus was of the same nature or substance as the Father. The Greek word for this is *homoousios*. In these English transliterations of the Greek words, we see that the words are very similar, differing in spelling by just the letter i. We see the same spelling similarity in Greek - ηομοιουσιος and ηομοουσιος. In Greek, the difference is the Greek letter *iota* - ι. This is the smallest letter of the Greek alphabet. At the time of the Arian controversy, culminating in the Council of Nicea, there were those who considered that the argument was not worthwhile, as it seemed to be arguing over nothing more than a tiny letter - ι. This has given rise to our phrase "it doesn't make an iota of difference". However, this particular iota makes a huge difference. A tiny difference in spelling represents an enormous difference in meaning. So Athanasius used his creed to emphasize that Jesus is "God, of the substance of the Father". He also emphasizes that Jesus was begotten, but that this was "before the worlds", so that the word begotten, as explained above, refers not to a starting time for Jesus, but merely to a hierarchy within the Trinity.

> ...and man of the substance of his mother, born in the world

This line emphasizes the humanity of Jesus, pointing out that he was genuinely human. Though, notice that Athanasius rightly emphasizes that Jesus was the substance of His mother, not His earthly father Joseph. This is akin to His foretelling as being the "seed of the woman" in Genesis 3:15.

> born in the world; perfect God and perfect man, of a rational soul and human flesh subsisting. Equal to the Father, as touching His godhead; and inferior to the Father, as touching His manhood

Athanasius emphasizes that Jesus' humanity and divinity were and are both perfect. Therefore, He could not be 50% God and 50% man. In other words, He must be 100% God and 100% man. Athanasius emphasizes this, together with the Trinitarian hierarchy - that Jesus is "equal to the Father, as touching His godhead; and inferior to the Father, as touching His manhood".

> who, although He is God and man, yet he is not two, but one Christ; one, not by conversion of the godhead into flesh but by taking of the manhood into God; one altogether; not by confusion of substance, but by unity of person.

The fact that Jesus is 100% God and 100% man requires us to emphasize that He is just one Person.

Athanasius does so in this section, and then goes on to relate a brief account of Jesus' life, thus showing that we cannot really understand the life and work of Jesus without accepting this concept of *Hypostatic Union.*

The definition that Athanius gives perhaps goes some way to explaining why the doctrine is given such a strange title. The Greek term *hypostasis* refers to natures. Thus, the doctrine teaches that Jesus has two natures, is 100% God and 100% man, and that these two natures are presented in the One Person - thus Hypostatic Union.

The Deity of Christ proved in the New Testament

The number of passages that could be quoted, with relation to the deity of Christ in the New Testament, is huge. This section will merely be a very abbreviated and idiosyncratic selection of the passages.

Perhaps the one passage that emphasizes this truth more than any other is Hebrews 1. Hebrews 1, after all, collects and quotes a large number of Old Testament passages and refers them to Jesus.

God, who at various times and in various ways spoke in time past to the fathers by the prophets, has in these last days spoken to us by *His* Son, whom He has appointed heir of all things, through whom also He made the worlds; who being the brightness of *His* glory and the express image of His person, and upholding all things by the word of His power, when He had by Himself purged our sins, sat down at the right hand of the Majesty on high, having become so much better than the angels, as He has by inheritance obtained a more excellent name than they. For to which of the angels did He ever say:

"You are My Son, today I have begotten You"? (Psalm 2)

And again:

"I will be to Him a Father, and He shall be to Me a Son"? (2 Samuel 7:14)

But when He again brings the firstborn into the world, He says:

"Let all the angels of God worship Him." (Deuteronomy 32:43)

And of the angels He says:

"Who makes His angels spirits and His ministers a flame of fire." (Psalm 104:4)

But to the Son He says:

"Your throne, O God, is forever and ever; a scepter of righteousness is the scepter of Your kingdom. You have loved righteousness and hated lawlessness; therefore God, Your God, has anointed You with the oil of gladness more than Your companions." (Psalm 45:6-7)

And:

"You, LORD, in the beginning laid the foundation of the earth, and the heavens are the work of Your hands. They will perish, but You remain; and they will all grow old like a garment; like a cloak You will fold them up, and they will be changed. But You are the same, and Your years will not fail." (Psalm 102:25a-27)

But to which of the angels has He ever said:

"Sit at My right hand, till I make Your enemies Your footstool"? (Psalm 110:1)

Are they not all ministering spirits sent forth to minister for those who will inherit salvation?

This short chapter starts by emphasizing the divinity of Jesus - that He is the Creator. Then, in a series of quotations from the Old Testament, the writer shows that Jesus is the one prophesied in the various messianic passages. Psalm 45, for example, is speaking to God - "Your throne, O God", yet the One being addressed in Psalm 45 is blessed by God (Psalm 45:3). So, Psalm 45 is addressed to someone who is blessed BY God, but who is Himself addressed as God. Yet the Bible makes clear there are not two Gods. Therefore, these are two persons of the same, One God.

But all of this might be irrelevant, if we didn't know that Jesus considered Himself to be God. It would take pages and hours to catalogue all the evidence that Jesus considered Himself to be God. Here are a few pointers.

Jesus applied the divine name of God to Himself.

> Then the Jews said to Him, "You are not yet fifty years old, and have You seen Abraham?" Jesus said to them, "Most assuredly, I say to you, before Abraham was, I AM." (John 8:57-58)

Some religious groups, such as the Jehovah's Witnesses, have tried to reword this verse, claiming it is bad grammar. However, the grammar is actually very clear, and is an explicit reference to God's revelation of His divine name, in Exodus 3:14.

> And God said to Moses, "I AM WHO I AM." And He said, "Thus you shall say to the children of Israel, 'I AM has sent me to you.'" (Exodus 3:14)

The phrase "I AM" is, in fact, the word often rendered as *YHWH*, or sometimes as *Jehovah*, and referred to as the Tetragrammaton, because it contains four Hebrew letters (יהוה). In English translations, it is usually rendered as LORD, with 4 capital letters. The use of the phrase "I am" was studiously avoided where possible by Jewish rabbis, but Jesus used the phrase elsewhere. When Jesus said

"I am the good shepherd. The good shepherd gives His life for the sheep." (John 10:11), his hearers would have understood that He was alluding to the 23rd Psalm - "The LORD (the I AM) is my shepherd" - and therefore applying it to Himself. We can make similar statements about the other well-known "I AM" statements of Jesus, such as "I am the door" (John 10:9) and "I am the resurrection and the life" (John 11:25).

When Jesus said "Before Abraham was, I AM", the Jews knew exactly what Jesus was claiming. In John 8:59 we read that they picked up stones to stone Him. This was also their reaction, with all the things that Jesus said in John 10. Note that in John 10, as well as saying "I am the good shepherd", Jesus said "I and My Father are one". Stoning was the punishment for blasphemy. They had reason for suggesting blasphemy. They knew that Jesus was claiming to be God. That would be a blasphemous claim - unless it were true, which it is!

It is also blasphemous for anyone to claim worship for themselves. Yet Jesus allowed worship of Himself on a number of occasions.

The earliest example of Jesus being worshipped is in Matthew 2:2, when the wise men arrive to worship Him. If this were an isolated example, it could be claimed that an infant would not be able to prevent false worship, but this is just the first of a number of occasions, many of which Jesus had the opportunity to repudiate, but did not.

> Then those who were in the boat came and worshiped Him, saying, "Truly You are the Son of God." (Matthew 14:33)

> And as they went to tell His disciples, behold, Jesus met them, saying, "Rejoice!" So they came and held Him by the feet and worshiped Him. (Matthew 28:9)

> Jesus heard that they had cast him out; and when He had found him, He said to him, "Do you believe in the Son of God?" He answered and said, "Who is He, Lord, that I may believe in Him?" And Jesus

said to him, "You have both seen Him and it is He who is talking with you." Then he said, "Lord, I believe!" And he worshiped Him. (John 9:35-38)

Note also the implication of what Jesus said to the man who He healed of a legion of demons.

[Jesus] said to him, "Go home to your friends, and tell them what great things the **Lord** has done for you, and how He has had compassion on you." And he departed and began to proclaim in Decapolis all that **Jesus** had done for him. (Mark 5:19-20, emphasis mine).

Jesus tells the man to tell everyone what the Lord had done for him - so he went and told everyone what **Jesus** had done for him. As far as the man formerly known as Legion was concerned, Jesus was the Lord. And nothing in the narrative or the words of Jesus corrects this - because both know it is true.

The Deity of Christ shown in the Old Testament

There are a number of passages in the Old Testament which are taken to refer to the coming

Messiah. Some of these passages show that the Messiah is Himself to be God. Some of the most important ones are those quoted in Hebrews 1, as discussed above. But there are others.

Psalm 2 was mentioned in Hebrews, but there is a lot more to this remarkable Messianic Psalm.

> The kings of the earth set themselves, And the rulers take counsel together, Against the LORD and against His Anointed. (Psalm 2:2)

The Anointed is in Hebrew *mâshîyah* (משיח), or Messiah. Yet this Messiah is to be honored as "the King". This King is to be "the Son" and He is to be kissed - a reference to worship.

The well-known prophecy of Micah concerning the birth of Jesus in Bethlehem reminds us that, although He is to be born in Bethlehem, His "goings forth are from of old, from everlasting." (Micah 5:2)

Jeremiah shows that the coming Messiah would be a human descendent of David, yet would be called by the divine name of God.

> "Behold, the days are coming," says the LORD, "That I will raise to David a Branch of righteousness; A King shall reign and prosper, And execute judgment and righteousness in the earth. In His days Judah will be saved, And Israel will dwell safely; Now this is His name by which He will be called: the LORD our righteousness." (Jeremiah 23:5-6)

It is no exaggeration to say that this section could be extended for page after page, tabulating all the various prophecies about the coming Messiah. For now, we will conclude this section, by showing how the idea of the Messiah or Second Person of the Trinity being God is essential to understanding Genesis, and clearly implied in the first book of the Bible.

The Deity of Christ in Genesis

In our discussion of the Trinity, in chapter 1, we saw how the presence of Jesus as the Second Person of the Trinity is implied even in Genesis 1. Bearing in mind that Jesus is described as "the image of the invisible God" (Colossians 1:15), we have to wonder who it was (of the Trinity) who was walking in the Garden in

Genesis 3:8. In order to be able to walk, it is not too big a leap to suggest that this is in fact God in human form - Jesus. John Bunyan certainly assumed this to be referring to Jesus.

> This voice John calls the word, the word that was with the Father before he made the world, and that at this very time was heard to walk in the garden of Adam.[16]

Realizing that the divine speaker in Genesis 3 is the Second Person of the Trinity puts a new light puts a new light on what is being said, especially in the well-known protoevangelium passage of Genesis 3:15.

> And I will put enmity between you and the woman, and between your seed and her Seed; He shall bruise your head, and you shall bruise His heel. (Genesis 3:15)

If you are not convinced of the argument that I am making, please try the tactic of assuming that I am correct that this speaker is actually Jesus, and see

---

[16] Bunyan, J. (2010), *Genesis: An Exposition of Chapters 1 to 11*, (Leicestershire: Just Six Days Publications), p73

where that assumption leads. You will see that important truths about Jesus are underlined by so doing.

Genesis 3:15 has traditionally been known as the protoevangelium, because it is widely taken as being the first declaration of the Gospel. In this verse, God (and, as I say, I take this to be specifically the Second Person of the Trinity) is speaking to the Serpent, and pronouncing a curse of him. But the substance of the verse is actually spoken for the benefit of Adam and Eve, who are stood listening, awaiting their own curse. The enmity between the serpent and the woman refers to the fact that Satan is the enemy of mankind - he is to be the enemy of all the descendents of the woman. The seed of the serpent are those who follow his way. They are not literally physically descended from him, as some have heretically suggested. Jesus pointed out that those who rejected Him were children of the devil in John 8:44. Yet the seed of the woman IS a real descendent, because we are talking about human descent. Yet how can someone be the seed of the woman? In Hebrew, "seed" refers to the descendent of a man. And biologically the seed is from the man. Bearing in mind everything else we know about Jesus from the scriptures, this would seem to imply that the person being referred to would have an earthly mother, but would not have an earthly father. Therefore, it would be a Virgin Birth! This seed of the woman can only be referring to Jesus, especially as He is the one who will crush or bruise the head of the serpent, thus destroying the serpent. If this is the Second Person of the Trinity talking - and He is, after all, the Word - the He is promising that He Himself will be the one to crush the serpent, by taking on human form. Bunyan puts it this:

> "It shall bruise thy head." By head, we are to understand the whole power, subtilty, and destroying nature of the devil; for as in the head of the serpent lieth his power, subtilty, and poisonous nature; so in sin, death, hell, and the wisdom of the flesh, lieth the very strength of the devil himself. Take away sin then, and death is not hurtful: "The sting of death is sin": And take away the condemning power of the law, and sin doth cease to be charged, or to have any more hurt in it,

so as to destroy the soul: "The strength of sin is the law" (1 Cor 15:56). Wherefore, the seed, Jesus Christ, in his bruising the head of the serpent, must take away sin, abolish death, and conquer the power of the grave. But how must this be done? Why, he must remove the curse, which makes sin intolerable, and death destructive. But how must he take away the curse? Why, by taking upon Him "flesh," as we (John 1:14); by being made "under the law," as we (Gal 4:4); by being made "to be sin for us" (2 Cor 5:21), and by being "made a curse for us" (Gal 3:10-13). He standing therefore in our room, under the law and the justice of God, did both bear, and overcome the curse, and so did bruise the power of the devil.[17]

Evidence for this would seem to be available at the beginning of Genesis 4. It is a reasonable assumption to suppose that, hearing this protoevangelium, Adam and Eve believed and were saved. Therefore, I suggest that Eve was looking for the appearance of the seed of the woman who would save humanity. But in her inexperience, she misunderstood one aspect, not

[17] Reference 16, p88

realizing that another 4,000 years would elapse before the Savior appeared. Therefore, when she gave birth to Cain, she said "I have acquired a man from the LORD." (Genesis 4:1). Cain actually means *acquired*, so this pronouncement of Eve's must be significant, as far as her beliefs were concerned. There are some who have suggested that what she actually said was "I have acquired a man: the LORD" - in other words, she was assuming that her new baby, Cain, was actually the LORD. Although this would turn out not to be the case, it does at least show that Eve was convinced that God was to come in human form as our Savior. Martin Luther was of this opinion.

> With respect therefore to Eve's adhering so closely to the Divine promise, and her believing so firmly in the deliverance that should surely come through her Seed, in all that she did rightly. For, by that same faith in the "Seed" that was to come, all the saints of old were justified and sanctified. But with respect to the individual intended by the promise, she erred. She believed that it was Cain who should put an end to all those calamities into which Satan had hurled man by sin. This faith of

Eve, however, rested on a certain opinion of her own, without any sure sign, and without the sure Word.[18]

Moving on into Genesis 4, we are presented with the account of Cain and Abel. I have written on this extensively before.[19,20] It is always important to realize that the entire point about Genesis 4 will not be understood, unless we realize that Abel's death is the first ever death of a human being. The whole impact of the account is lost, if Adam and Eve were preceded by millions of years of human evolution, with death, disease and suffering. In my book, *Cain and Abel*, I have shown:

1. Jesus described Abel as a prophet

---

[18] Luther, M. *The Creation: A Commentary on the First Five Chapters of Genesis*, < http://www.ebooksread.com/authors-eng/martin-luther/the-creation--a-commentary-on-the-first-five-chapters-of-the-book-of-genesis-htu/page-34-the-creation--a-commentary-on-the-first-five-chapters-of-the-book-of-genesis-htu.shtml >, accessed September 15th 2010

[19] See Taylor, P. (2007) *The Six Days of Creation*, (Green Forest, AR: Master Books), pp115-127

[20] See also Taylor, P. (2009) *Cain and Abel: Worship and Sacrifice*, (Leicestershire: Just Six Days Publications)

2. We have no record of any prophetic words of Abel.

3. Abel's prophecy is, in fact, his shed blood.

Therefore, we see that the shedding of the first ever human blood is a *type*[21] of the shedding of human blood already prophesied in Genesis 3:15. Included with this is the fact that Abel's occupation as a keeper of sheep could not have been in order to provide meat, as the eating of meat was not sanctioned until after the Flood. Therefore, his occupation was to provide skins as clothing, to cover nakedness and guilt -just as God clothed Adam and Eve with skins, thereby shedding

[21] The website GotQuestions.com defines *type* and *typology* thus: "Typology is a special kind of symbolism. (A symbol is something which represents something else.) We can define a type as a "prophetic symbol" because all types are representations of something yet future. More specifically, a type in scripture is a person or thing in the Old Testament which foreshadows a person or thing in the New Testament.... When we say that someone is a type of Christ, we are saying that a person in the Old Testament behaves in a way that corresponds to Jesus' character or actions in the New Testament. When we say that something is 'typical' of Christ, we are saying that an object or event in the Old Testament can be viewed as representative of some quality of Jesus.", < http://www.gotquestions.org/typology-Biblical.html >, accessed September 15th 2010

the first ever animal blood, in order to cover Adam and Eve's guilt. Thus, Jesus' humanity is seen in His comparison with Abel, and His deity is seen as the fulfillment of the type.

Genesis continues with countless other examples of the deity of Christ, such as the appearance of the LORD to Abraham, to reveal more of the plan of salvation to him, especially through Abraham's line of descent through Isaac. This explains how Abraham could be saved by faith; "And Abram believed in the LORD, and He accounted it to him for righteousness." (Genesis 15:6)

Conclusion

In this study, we have looked at the biblical reasons for believing Jesus to be both God and man. We have seen that His nature can be described as human and as divine, yet He is not 50% human and 50% divine - He is 100% human and 100% divine. This dual nature understanding of Jesus is known as the Hypostatic Union. Furthermore, we have seen that an attempt to downplay either the human or the divine nature of

Jesus simply leads to error and heresy. The Hypostatic Union is seen throughout the New Testament, but can also be understood with reference to the Old Testament, including the foundational book of Genesis.

Inerrancy of Scripture

The inerrancy of scripture is at the heart of what evangelicals believe. Though the concept is under attack today, in contexts which would previously have been thought of as evangelical, it is noteworthy that the major statements of faith include comments on the place of scripture. Terms associated with the place of scripture include *inerrancy, authority* and *infallibility*. It is important to be clear what we mean by these terms. It is also important to realize that they do not refer to three different aspects of our understanding of scripture, which could be adopted separately. Although they have different meanings, inerrancy implies authority and authority implies infallibility etc.

Inerrancy

To say that the Bible is inerrant is to say that it is without error. The Chicago Statement on Biblical Inerrancy[1] puts it thus:

---

[1] < http://www.bible-researcher.com/chicago1.html >

We affirm that Scripture in its entirety is inerrant,
being free from all falsehood, fraud, or deceit.

This is a problematic statement for some, as they
appeal to the various translations that have been
made over the years and suggest that copyists' errors
might have been made. The Chicago Statement has
something to say on that issue.

We affirm that inspiration, strictly speaking,
applies only to the autographic text of Scripture,
which in the providence of God can be ascertained
from available manuscripts with great accuracy.
We further affirm that copies and translations of
Scripture are the Word of God to the extent that
they faithfully represent the original.

We deny that any essential element of the
Christian faith is affected by the absence of the
autographs. We further deny that this absence
renders the assertion of Biblical inerrancy invalid
or irrelevant.

What is being stated is that, although there could be
errors of translation, we have sufficient stable well-

researched manuscripts to be sure that an accurate translation can be made, which, in turn, increases our confidence in the Bible's inerrancy.

Authority

A document which can be claimed to be inerrant, that gives instructions on how one might be saved, will be endowed with a unique authority. That document is the Bible, claiming, as it does, to be the inspired word of God. That inspiration of God endows the Bible with a unique authority.

Many official Statements of Faith (SoF) require this level of biblical authority. For example, the SoF of the Assemblies of God (UK) states:

> We believe that the Bible (i.e. the Old and New Testaments excluding the Apocrypha), is the inspired Word of God, the infallible, all sufficient rule for faith and practice.[2]

The AoG SoF quotes scripture verses with its articles. The article about the Bible – which is the first article – lists the verses 2 Timothy 3:15-16 and 2 Peter 1:21. The

---

[2] < http://www.aog.org.uk/pages/17-statement-of-faith/content >

import of these verses will be discussed later. Although this article does not explicitly use the word authority, this is implied by the use of the phrase ("all sufficient rule").

The SoF of the Fellowship of Independent Evangelical Churches (FIEC) states:

> God has revealed himself in the Bible, which consists of the Old and New Testaments alone. Every word was inspired by God through human authors, so that the Bible as originally given is in its entirety the Word of God, without error and fully reliable in fact and doctrine. The Bible alone speaks with final authority and is always sufficient for all matters of belief and practice.[3]

The FIEC's article emphasizes inerrancy, authority and sufficiency of the Bible. These three would seem to imply infallibility.

Infallibility

Infallibility implies that, not only is the Bible without error, but it speaks without fault. This quality

---

[3] < www.fiec.org.uk >

is implied by SoFs that speak about the sufficiency of scripture. Sufficiency means that all doctrine can be determined from within the pages of scripture, without having to add external ideas. This is not to say that no external literature is ever consulted. If any ideas external to scripture are adopted, it would only be because these ideas were supported by scripture, s that they would not actually be ideas external to scripture. This explains why evangelical groups can quote evangelical authors, on the understanding that their work is itself based on the sufficiency of scripture.

It is usually understood that these terms work together. In theory, it could be supposed that scripture might be infallible but not inerrant. Evangelicals deny that possibility. Scripture's infallibility is dependent on its inerrancy. Likewise, there are those who lend an authority to scripture, without accepting infallibility. Evangelicals also deny this possibility.

The Scriptural Basis for Inerrancy

The Bible argues for its own inerrancy, authority and infallibility. Two good starting points for seeing this internal argument in practice are the verses quoted with the AoG SoF.

> From childhood you have known the Holy Scriptures, which are able to make you wise for salvation through faith which is in Christ Jesus. All Scripture *is* given by inspiration of God, and *is* profitable for doctrine, for reproof, for correction, for instruction in righteousness, that the man of God may be complete, thoroughly equipped for every good work. (2 Timothy 3:15-17)

Paul commends Timothy for knowing the scriptures. He describes these scriptures as "holy" – which means "set apart" – literally, set apart for God. Paul tells Timothy that the scriptures are there to make him wise. So his wisdom is not to come from external sources, but only to be based on scripture. This wisdom is "for salvation through faith". Our basis for our faith is to be found only in scripture. The fact that this is "in Christ Jesus" emphasizes that our knowledge of Christ Himself is to be found in scripture. It should be noted that the scripture, to which Paul is here referring, is the scripture of his time – i.e. the Old Testament. So this verse emphasizes the inerrancy, infallibility and authority of the Old Testament. It will then be necessary to see if we can apply this verse to the New Testament also.

Paul refers to "all scripture" being "inspired". Therefore, there is not a part of the OT which is not inspired (and our further studies will apply this to the NT). If it is inspired, then it is the Holy Spirit who has spoken through it. Therefore, although different books were written by different authors, it was the one Holy Spirit who inspired their writing. Inspiration is not dictation. The styles of the different authors were not subverted by the Holy Spirit. But nor is inspiration just a vague kind of influence. Inspiration implies that all scripture is from God – indeed it is His word.

Finally, in this section, Paul explains the use of scripture. It is there to provide us with all our doctrine or teaching; it is there to rebuke us and correct us when we are going astray; and it is there for our instruction. It is only with scripture, and our adherence to and knowledge of it, that we can be "complete" or "thoroughly equipped for every good work".

> No prophecy of Scripture is of any private interpretation, for prophecy never came by the will of man, but holy men of God spoke *as they were* moved by the Holy Spirit. (2 Peter 1:19-21)

In the previous passage, Paul laid down the implications of inspiration. In this passage, Peter explains **how** inspiration came about. Scripture comes by prophecy. This does not imply that all prophecy is scripture. For example, we do not have a record of the words of the prophets in the cave (1 Kings 18:4). The theology of prophecy is not appropriate to the current discussion. Nevertheless, we can state that all scripture is prophecy – and that it is all that is necessary for our life and work. To say that it is prophetic implies that it came directly from God. Yet Peter acknowledges that it is written by human hand –

yet he emphasizes that these human hands "were moved by the Holy Spirit".

Once again, we are being told about the Old Testament scripture. Historic documents make it very clear that the Old Testament Canon was known and complete very soon indeed after the completion of its writing, about 400BC. However, Peter goes on to add some of the New Testament writings to his definition of scripture.

> Therefore, beloved, looking forward to these things, be diligent to be found by Him in peace, without spot and blameless; and consider *that* the longsuffering of our Lord *is* salvation—as also **our beloved brother Paul**, according to the wisdom given to him, has written to you, as also in **all his epistles**, speaking in them of these things, in which are some things hard to understand, which untaught and unstable *people* twist to their own destruction, **as *they do* also the rest of the Scriptures**. (2 Peter 3: 14-16 emphasis mine)

Peter is here acknowledging that Paul is his beloved brother. Why is Paul "our beloved brother". In one sense, Peter is speaking for himself and his readers. But it is not too far a stretch to suggest that Peter is also including Paul among the brethren of the apostles. Since Paul includes himself as such in his epistles, Peter's inclusion of "all his epistles" is also an endorsement of Paul's apostleship. Finally, we should note that Peter talks about "the rest of the scriptures" – clearly endorsing Paul's epistles as scripture. This passage could also be taken slightly more broadly, and be seen as an implicit endorsement as scripture of the genuinely scriptural writings of other apostles (e.g. Matthew and John), as well as those under direct apostolic authority. Popular theologian, Brian Edwards, has written at length on why we should accept all 27 NT books (and no others) as being Canonical.

The Canon of Scripture

On a number of occasions in this discussion, I have used the words *canon* or *canonical*. These words are used to describe whether a book is truly biblical or not. The etymology of the word *canon* is from the word for *rule* – implying not a law but rather a way of doing things. I wrote previously about the use of the word *canon* in the *New Answers Book 2*, as follows:

> We have become quite used to the word *canon* these days. The word is frequently used of a body of literature. For example, one can refer to the complete works of Shakespeare as the *Shakespearian* canon. More bizarrely, I recently read a discussion about whether certain novels about *Doctor Who* could be considered to be part of the Doctor Who *canon*. Strangely, this last usage was closer to the correct use of the word *canon*, as applied to Scripture. The argument went that the novels introduced concepts and ideas that were later contradicted or not found to be in harmony with events reported in the recent revised TV series. Presumably, the writer of the article felt that these *Doctor Who* novels were not following an accepted rule or pattern.[4]

The books previously footnoted by Brian Edwards discuss in great detail why the 66 books of the Bible are included in the canon and why others are not. A study

---

[4] Taylor, P.F., *Is the Bible Enough?*, in Ham, K. (ed.) (2008), *New Answers Book 2*, (Green Forest, AR: Master Books), pp219-220

of the accepted canon of scripture is very helpful in underlining the inerrancy, sufficiency and authority of scripture.

Casting Doubt on God's Word

Having accepted the whole Bible as authoritative, inerrant, infallible and sufficient, we can see that a failure to accept any part of scripture is a failure to believe God Himself. This does not mean that honest Bible-believing people will not sometimes disagree on the interpretation of parts of scripture – though these disagreements will center on secondary issues, rather than the primary issues, essential to our faith. It is interesting to note that, in the opinion of this writer, the common objections to the acceptance of scripture as God's word are seen in the very first temptation and sin, found in Genesis 3.

Genesis 3 is about the temptation of Eve by Satan, the sin of Adam, God's curse on Satan, Adam and creation and the promise of redemption.

The Serpent of Genesis 3 is identified in Revelation 12 as the devil or Satan.

> So the great dragon was cast out, that serpent of old, called the Devil and Satan, who deceives the whole world; he was cast to the earth, and his angels were cast out with him. (Revelation 12:9)

In Genesis 3, he is described as being "cunning".

> Now the serpent was more cunning than any beast of the field which the LORD God had made. (Genesis 3:1)

This verse emphasizes that Satan was created. The text is not referring to serpents in general, but to this particular serpent – i.e. Satan. His "cunning" is referred to as "craftiness" in 2 Corinthians 11.

> But I fear, lest somehow, as the serpent deceived Eve by his craftiness, so your minds may be corrupted from the simplicity that is in Christ. (2 Corinthians 11:3)

This "craftiness" is contrasted with the simplicity of Christian doctrine "that is in Christ". The KJV uses the concept of "subtlety" in both the above passages. In both cases, the implication is that a twisting of scripture has occurred. How can this be, when in

Genesis 3 no written scripture yet existed? The answer lies in the acknowledgment that scripture is the word of God. Therefore, God's previous words to Adam have the authority of scripture. The key words, on which the events of Genesis 3 rest, are to be found in chapter 2.

> And the LORD God commanded the man, saying, "Of every tree of the garden you may freely eat; but of the tree of the knowledge of good and evil you shall not eat, for in the day that you eat of it you shall surely die." (Genesis 2:16-17)

These verses give a command to Adam, and the consequences for not obeying that command. The fact that the command is given suggests that God had made Adam with the capability of obedience or disobedience. In order for Adam to exercise obedience, he had to have a command, which it was possible for him to disobey. Therefore, the command involved not eating a particular fruit. It should be noted that there was almost certainly nothing inherently poisonous about the fruit. It was not the fruit that led to Adam's death – it was his disobedience toward God. This disobedience – a breaking of a commandment – is what the Bible refers to as sin.

God told Adam that there would be a consequence for disobedience. He said that "the day that you eat of it you shall surely die". What sort of death happened? Adam didn't appear to fall dead on the spot. For this reason, some have suggested that Adam's death was "spiritual" rather than literal. The theistic evolutionist, Denis Alexander, says this about the events of Genesis 3:

> "The failure of Adam and Eve to physically drop dead on the *yom* [day] that they disobeyed God highlights once again the need to interpret the meanings of words by their context. Here in Genesis 3 the passage is quite clear that Adam and Eve died as a result of their sin, just as God warned, *but they died spiritually.*"[5]

---

[5] Alexander, D.R. (2008), *Creation or Evolution: Do we have to choose?*, (Oxford: Monarch), p261, emphasis mine

In his masterful review and refutation of Alexander's ideas, David Anderson writes:

> Dr. Alexander achieves these conclusions mostly by continuing to interpret Genesis overall as a "theological and figurative"... narrative, and by interpreting other relevant biblical passages through the false dichotomy of "spiritual death" versus "physical death". This is carried on even when dealing with passages such as 1 Corinthians 15, where the physical resurrection from physical death is stage front and center – even then, it never seems to really dawn on Dr. Alexander to see that this dualistic separation is fundamentally un- and anti-biblical.[6]

Alexander is incorrect to make a point about Adam failing to drop dead the same day that he ate the fruit. Dr Terry Mortenson has pointed out that the biblical phrase "surely die" does not mean immediate death. The same phrase occurs in Numbers 26:65.

---

[6] Anderson, D. (2008), *Creation or Evolution: Why we must choose*, (Leicestershire: J6D Publications), p112

> For the LORD had said of them, "They shall surely
> die in the wilderness." So there was not left a man
> of them, except Caleb the son of Jephunneh and
> Joshua the son of Nun.

In the passage from Numbers, it is clear that the
death is not to be immediate. Moreover, the Genesis
2:17 passage does not imply a 24-hour day. Alexander
is deliberately mixing his contexts for this purpose. In
Genesis 2:17, *yom* (day) is not accompanied by a
number, or the words evening, morning or night. All
6-day creationists acknowledge that the word *yom* **can**
mean something other than a 24-hour day – it just
can't mean something other than a 24-hour day when
used with a number, evening, morning or night. See
Numbers 7, for example, and decide whether the
events of Numbers 7 could have taken place over 12
literal days or 12,000 years.

Mortenson goes on to suggest this about the phrase
"you shall surely die".

> The phrase "you shall surely die" can be literally
> translated from the Hebrew Biblical text as "dying

you shall die." In the Hebrew phrase we find the imperfect form of the Hebrew verb (you shall die) with the infinitive absolute form of the same verb (dying). This presence of the infinitive absolute intensifies the meaning of the imperfect verb (hence the usual translation of "you shall surely die").[7]

What this means is that God's word did not tell Adam that he would drop dead the very same day that he disobeyed God's command. Instead, it means that the **process** of death would start immediately and be inevitable from that moment. Adam lived for a further 930 years. That sounds like a long time. But when you remember that Adam was designed to live forever, 930 years does not sound so long after all.

It is interesting that the objection to a literal interpretation of Genesis 2:17 has a great deal of

[7] Mortenson, T. (2007), *Genesis 2:17 - "You shall surely die"*, < http://www.answersingenesis.org/articles/2007/05/02/dying-you-shall-die >

resonance with the objection to God's word conjured by the serpent in Genesis 3.

> And he said to the woman, "Has God indeed said, 'You shall not eat of every tree of the garden'?" (Genesis 3:1)

It is quite useful to deconstruct what Satan is doing here. First, we notice that he spoke to the woman, not to the man. Yet God's command, while being in place for all humanity, was originally delivered to the man. Satan therefore tackled the person who had received the command second-hand. This is not to excuse Eve's subsequent errors – she should have accepted the information from Adam fully. We should also note that Genesis 3:6 suggests that Adam was with her. There are those who would suggest – and I count myself among them – that Adam was actually a witness to the entire deception of Eve, yet said nothing during their conversation. It must be noted that there are many commentators who disagree with the point I have just made but, if it were correct, it would add to the joint failure of Adam and Eve to accept fully the word of God. We can fall for the same trick. If our adherence to God's word is only second-hand, we will be susceptible to Satan's attacks. For this reason, and for many other reasons, we need to read the Bible for ourselves, being fully immersed in it.

The second point about Satan's initial temptation is his phrasing. He puts the commandment negatively. God's commandment in Genesis 2:16 was positive – "Of every tree of the garden you may freely eat" – with a negative injunction for the fruit of one tree only. Satan is a master of the concept that the media is the message. By phrasing the command negatively, he tries to make God out to be mean – a spoilsport, out to ruin Adam and Eve's pleasure. The positive command shows the abundant care that God has for the people He has created. Satan tries to imply that God does not care for His people, nor lavish His love on them, whereas Genesis 2:16 – with its huge and wide-ranging permission to eat all sorts of different fruits – illustrates an abundance of love and care, over and above what we need. Throughout scripture, we read of God's lavish love for us, yet it is the devil's trick to try to persuade us that God does not care for our particular situation. God gives us rules and laws for our protection, because He cares for us, but too often we portray such biblical morality as a hindrance to our freedom.

Third, we should notice that Satan places the command in a question, in order to cast doubt on God's word. "Has God indeed said...", or, as the NLT puts it, "Did God really say...", requires us to consider whether God really said this or not. It becomes a test of our ability to discern the mind of God from scripture. The theistic evolutions, like Dr. Alexander, fall short at this very point. Alexander says "the biblical understanding of creation is not primarily concerned with how things began, but why they exist." Yet Genesis 1 explicitly claims to be an account of **how** God made the world, and doesn't actually state **why** God made it. Another theistic evolutionist said, in debate with me, "we need to understand what the actual purpose of Genesis is". In their minds, the purpose of Genesis is not historical narrative. Yet the plain meaning of the text actually **is** historical narrative. So, if we read what the words actually say, the theistic evolutionists think we should filter our reading of the word through their presupposition of how the world began. It is as if they are saying "Did God really say He made the world in six 24-hour periods? Actually, He meant millions of years." "Did God really say…" is the preface to the world's oldest lie and the world's oldest temptation. And the theistic evolutionists – even those who claim, as Alexander does, to believe "the Bible as the authoritative Word of God" – are actually echoing that deception of the devil.

And the woman said to the serpent, "We may eat the fruit of the trees of the garden; but of the fruit of the tree which *is* in the midst of the garden, God has said, 'You shall not eat it, nor shall you touch it, lest you die.'" (Genesis 3:2)

Having analyzed Satan's first deception, we now look at Eve's reply. There is a good point and a bad point about Eve's reply. The good point is that Eve picked up on the main accusation Satan made against God – that He was mean and unfair in restricting their choice of fruit. She countered Satan with a repeat of the positive mode, in which God placed the command "we **may** eat...". However, the source of her error – and eventual downfall – is detected in her report of God's command. She misquotes what God said. Indeed, she added to what God said: "'You shall not eat it, nor shall you touch it, lest you die'". She had added the phrase "nor shall you touch it". God had not forbidden them from touching the fruit – only from eating it. This is the reason why God tells us throughout scripture not to add to His words.

> Do not add to His words, Lest He rebuke you, and you be found a liar. (Proverbs 30:6)

To some extent, it is not a surprise that Eve got her ideas mixed up. Perhaps her first error was to engage Satan in conversation at all. Our reaction, when it is intimated to us that we should doubt God, should be to turn away from the Tempter – "Get behind me Satan" – rather than to discuss the issue. There was no way, for example, that Eve was going to persuade Satan that God's law was just.

Having succeeded in disturbing Eve's adherence to God's word, Satan comes in with a second strategy.

> Then the serpent said to the woman, "You will not surely die. For God knows that in the day you eat of it your eyes will be opened, and you will be like God, knowing good and evil." (Genesis 3:4-5)

Satan's next comment is a direct contradiction of what God said – "You will not surely die". In resisting temptation, it is important to note that Satan does not usually start by contradicting God. But he will certainly end up there. His strategy in Genesis 3 is a common one.

i.   He casts doubt on what God says.

ii. He watches for us misquoting God.

iii. He contradicts God.

Satan suggests to Eve that knowing good and evil would be a desirable end. It would make them, he suggests, like God. Satan's comment in verse 5 is suggesting that God is deliberately concealing something from Adam and Eve that would give them power; withholding something that would do them 'good'.

Even at this stage, it would have been possible for Adam and Eve not to sin. It is not inevitable that they should follow Satan's strategy. Moreover, the New Testament reminds us that Eve's sin was her own, but that Adam was not taken in by Satan – yet he still sinned, thereby passing his original sin down to all his heirs – including you and me.

> And Adam was not deceived, but the woman being deceived, fell into transgression. (1 Timothy 2:14)

So the whole pattern for doubting the inerrancy of the Bible was set here in Genesis 3. We don't know when the events of Genesis 3 happened – though it is most likely that Genesis 3 occurred soon after the creation week. Archbishop Ussher suggests that these events happened on the very same day that Adam and Eve were brought into the Garden of Eden – which he suggests would be Day 10. His reason for choosing this date is that, if it were so, then the Day of Atonement (Leviticus 23:27) would fall on an anniversary of the event, which would make *Yom Kippur* doubly significant. (In parentheses, it can be noted that this dating is also part of the reason why so many of us take Ussher's chronology to be very accurately worked out, and not the object of ridicule, in which it is held by so many so-called scholars on the subject). Whether or not Ussher's chronology is correct, it would seem to make sense to place the events of Genesis 3 very soon after the Creation Week. And there is so much more to say on Genesis 3 – so we will need to revisit an exegesis of the chapter in our studies on 'Sin and Death' and 'The Gospel'.

Conclusion

The first temptation and the first sin involved a pattern of disbelief in the inerrancy of God's word – a direct analogue of our own times' disbelief in the inerrancy of scripture. God had given a clear and positive command, but with information about what the consequences of disobedience would be. Satan's temptation involved casting doubt on God's word, attacking a faulty knowledge of God's word, then directly contradicting God's word. This pattern is seen today in liberal churches, but also in churches and among scholars who we would hitherto have thought evangelical (and who frequently still call themselves evangelical).

Our earlier discussions – and the books referenced, especially those by Brian Edwards – remind us that a belief in the inerrancy of scripture is a rational and reasonable position to take, and is essential to give us any foundation for our beliefs and teachings.

Sin and Death

For the reader who is convinced that Genesis gives a historical account of events at creation, the doctrines of sin and death are inextricably linked. Unlike some of the other teachings discussed in this book, the best 'proof texts' for the topic are found in Genesis. In this case, then, it is not a matter of tracing the doctrine back to find its origins in Genesis. We would generally start with Genesis to derive the doctrine.

The purpose of this book, however, is to see how Genesis is the foundation for Christian teaching. For that reason, unusually for this doctrine, we will start by surveying its appearance in a small number of other places in scripture, before returning to Genesis. This will make the chapter match the others, and will emphasize the unity of scripture on all these important teachings.

What is sin?

"Sin is lawlessness" says the apostle John (1 John 3:4). In fact, John has a lot to say about sin in his first epistle

– an epistle that most people seem to think is exclusively about love! In the full quote from this verse, we read:

> Whoever commits sin also commits lawlessness, and sin is lawlessness. (1 John 3:4)

So sin is defined by reference to law – and John is specifically talking about the law of God. This is most succinctly put in the Ten Commandments. It is the failure to meet these commandments which is sin. Paul explains this in that great passage about the reason for the law, in Romans 7.

> What shall we say then? *Is* the law sin? Certainly not! On the contrary, I would not have known sin except through the law. For I would not have known covetousness unless the law had said, "*You shall not covet.*" (Romans 7:7)

John is very concerned about his readers' sinful nature. His epistle stresses the need not to sin.

> My little children, these things I write to you, so that you may not sin. And if anyone sins, we have

an Advocate with the Father, Jesus Christ the righteous. (1 John 2:1)

Note that John does not want his readers to sin. He is also realistic enough to know that they will. This leads to some apparent contradictions – which are, in fact, easily resolved.

Whoever abides in Him does not sin. Whoever sins has neither seen Him nor known Him. (1 John 3:6)

In the verse above, John shows that sin is an indicator that the sinner is not saved. If we are living in Him, then we do not sin. Yet, he also acknowledges that this is impossible.

If we say that we have no sin, we deceive ourselves, and the truth is not in us. (1 John 1:8)

The reconciliation of these facts is that we should be making every effort not to sin as part of our witness. However, we know that our sins are dealt with by Jesus. Those who deliberately sin have a major problem.

And you know that He was manifested to take away our sins, and in Him there is no sin. (1 John 3:5)

Paul, like John, reminds us that all have sinned.

All have sinned and fall short of the glory of God (Romans 3:23)

Isaiah says something similar, in that great prophetic passage about the Servant King.

All we like sheep have gone astray; We have turned, every one, to his own way; And the LORD has laid on Him the iniquity of us all. (Isaiah 53:6)

The Old and New Testaments therefore proclaim that sin is something which is at the heart of all people, without exception. It is suggested that this is a self-evident fact. The Bible also claims, in the same passages, to know where this sin came from and how it originated. As we shall see later, many passages claim that sin began because of Adam's disobedience. However, we will analyze that point, when we take the teaching back to its roots in Genesis.

Death is the Result of Sin

Sin does not go unpunished. This is an unpopular notion today. Words such as sin, bad or evil are taboo words. Even in education, it is politically incorrect to say "your behavior is naughty". If little Jim has pulled Mary's hair, then his behavior is deemed to be "inappropriate" – which suggests that pulling Mary's hair might be an appropriate response in different circumstances. That is not the way that God acts. Such a manner would be contrary to God's nature.

In Jeremiah, we read:

> Thus says the LORD: "Let not the wise *man* glory in his wisdom, Let not the mighty *man* glory in his might, Nor let the rich *man* glory in his riches; But let him who glories glory in this, That he understands and knows Me, That I *am* the LORD, exercising lovingkindness, judgment, and righteousness in the earth. For in these I delight," says the LORD. (Jeremiah 9:23-24)

In this passage, we read that there are three things in which God delights. These three things are "lovingkindness, judgment and righteousness in the earth." We need to follow through the logic of these verses. As human beings, we are told that we cannot glory in what seems to make us great or important - "Let not the wise *man* glory in his wisdom, Let not the mighty *man* glory in his might, Nor let the rich *man* glory in his riches". This is because none of these things match the glory of God. Instead, our "glory" is to be in understanding and knowing God. In order to understand and know God, we need to know His character. His character is revealed through His actions and through what he delights in. If you want to get to know someone better, then find out what they really enjoy doing. What really makes them tick. If this does not sound too irreverent, these verses tell us what makes God tick.

I suppose most people, trying to describe the attributes of God, would start with "God is love". This is, of course, true - though many might be surprised to find that this phrase, in its baldest form, occurs only once in the Bible.

He who does not love does not know God, for God is love. (1 John 4:8)

The trouble with simply quoting "God is love" - although, as I have said, it is definitely true - is that many people seem to think this sums up God completely. Therefore, their God becomes a liberal dispenser of everything that *they* wish to define as loving. This is what leads to the age-old question "How could a God of love send people to Hell?" Clark Pinnock[1] and John Stott[2] have both argued that impenitent souls do not end up in a place of eternal punishment, but are, rather, "annihilated". Pinnock says "everlasting torment is intolerable from a moral point of view because it makes God into a bloodthirsty monster who maintains an everlasting Auschwitz for victims whom He does not even allow to die. How is one to worship or imitate such a cruel and merciless

[1] Pinnock, C.H., *The Destruction of the Finally Impenitent*, A Journal from the Radical Reformation, Fall 1992, Vol. 2, No. 1. (1992), < http://www.abc-coggc.org/jrad/volume2/issue1/The%20Destruction%20of%20the%20Finally%20Impenitent.pdf >, accessed 3rd August 2010.

[2] John Stott, in Evangelical Essentials: A Liberal-Evangelical Dialogue, ed. David L. Edwards (Downers Grove, IL: InterVarsity, 1988), 315-16

God?"[3] Such views have been criticized by other evangelicals, however. Pinnock appears to be judging God by his own standards. After all, what definition can we possibly have of what a "moral point of view" might be, if we do not examine the doctrine of God from a scriptural standpoint? Millard J. Erickson has said:

> The idea of the wicked being obliterated rather than suffering endlessly will continue to appeal to sensitive Christians. Yet emotion cannot be the primary consideration in settling theological issues. In this case the biblical and theological data weigh strongly on the side of eternal conscious punishment of the wicked.[4]

The verses in Jeremiah quoted above help us to understand the nature of God in context. As we have seen, three attributes need to be understood together - "lovingkindness, judgment and righteousness in the

[3] Reference 1, p15

[4] Erickson, M.J., *Is Hell Forever?*, Bibliotheca Sacra 152: 607 (1995): 259-272, < http://www.theologicalstudies.org.uk/article_hell_erickson.html >, accessed 3rd August 2010.

earth." Lovingkindness has to be understood in the light of God's righteousness. God is most certainly love. But God is also righteousness. So it would not be righteous for God to wink at unrighteousness. Such an act would not be the lovingkindness sort of action that the Bible attributes to God. God's righteousness is displayed "in the earth". Again, it is not part of the action of a loving God, therefore, to ignore the wicked state of the world. So God assures us, through Jeremiah, that He is also the God of Judgment.

The Bible makes clear that the principle punishment for sin is death. In Romans 6:23, we read, "For the wages of sin is death, but the gift of God is eternal life in Christ Jesus our Lord." The contrast between the two clauses of this verse emphasizes the nature of the Gospel. Wages are paid as recompense for work done. I do not give my work freely (unless I am volunteering). My job provides me with a wage. This wage is earned by the work that I have done. Therefore, what we earn from a lifetime of sin - even from just one is sin - is death. This verse also explains why we cannot get to Heaven just by attempting to be good. Just one small sin earns us death, and, if we are honest with ourselves, we will realize that we have committed more than one small sin each. So if we achieve "eternal life in Christ Jesus our Lord", this cannot be earned by a wage. Rather, it is a gift - "the gift of God". It comes only from God, and by His divine election. Romans 6:23 is a clear application of the fact that the attributes of God are "lovingkindness, judgment and righteousness in the earth." His lovingkindness is seen in the fact that eternal life is a gift. His judgment is seen in the fact that sin earns death - and that sin, because of His righteousness, has to receive a real and lasting punishment. That death is the appropriate punishment for sin is illustrated by Romans 6, and indeed by 1 Corinthians 15:56. "The sting of death is sin, and the strength of sin is the law". A wasp sting has an effect, because of its venom. Death's sting has an effect - it causes us to die. And the sting of death is sin. Moreover, 1 Corinthians 15:56 reminds us that sin is, in fact, transgression of the law. This issue will be illustrated further later in the chapter, by means of an exposition of Genesis 3.

The Seriousness of Sin

The fact that sin leads to death should underline its seriousness. However, because of the unpalatable connotations of such teaching, there are those who have sought to undermine the seriousness of sin, usually by redefining it, or giving it another name. A standard orthodox presentation of the Gospel involves making sure that a person knows they are a sinner, so that they know they need a savior. This sin exists in every person: "All have sinned and fall short of the glory of God" (Romans 3:23)

Today, however, many churches have redefined sins as hurts. The big problem that people in the world have is that there are strongholds which need to be dismantled, rather than sins which need to be forgiven. This has led to a form of evangelism which seems to be more akin to psychiatry than to the Gospel of Jesus Christ.

Stephanie D. Miller, founder of the ministry "Kingdom Impactors"[5], describes these strongholds thus:

> *Strongholds are formed when things are present: unmet needs, unhealed hurts, and unresolved issues.* **Unmet needs** are birthed when something good that should have happened didn't. For example, parents were designed by God to love their children, protect then, and provide for them. When that doesn't happen, the child has unmet needs. **Wrong behaviors** form over the course of the child's life as a source of protection, a safe place, such as wrong relationships, sarcasm, and insubordination to authority figures caused by a lack of trust. **Unhealed hurts** are birthed when something bad that should not have happened did. Think about a teenager that gets pregnant by someone who said that he loved her and then he rejects her and she gets an abortion. An unhealed hurt may occur if not dealt with. Another example is a young teenage male is pulled over as the victim of racial profiling and has to strip down and

[5] < http://kingdomimpactors.com/about_us >

undergo hostile interrogation only to be released with no offer of an apology. Both of these are unhealed hurts that can result in behaviors such as denial, suspicion, victim mentality, and more. **Unresolved issues** are birthed when you are incapable of processing such occurrences in a positive spiritual, mental, emotional, and physical manner. The afflictions of a righteous man are many but God delivers us from them all. Some behaviors resulting from unresolved issues include rigidity, legalism, perfectionism, and workaholism. They all have at the root of them the need to be in control. Have you ever said these things before? They'll never make me cry again. I can take care of myself. I am the captain of my own ship. I don't need anyone to tell me anything; I'm just as smart as they are. You better prove it to me![6]

The article goes on to use scripture to describe the dismantling of strongholds, by looking at how strongholds were dismantled in the Bible. However, it is not clear that the Bible passages quoted refer to the

[6] Miller, S.D., *Strongholds: The Soul's Defense*, < http://kingdomimpactors.com/stronghold1_article061118.html >, accessed 4th August 2010

same sort of thing as being described in the article. I once attended a church, where the minister talked about people walking around the city center, full of unhealed hurts, and how we, as the church, needed to provide the healing. The trouble with such statements is that there may be an element of truth in them, but they miss the point. What separates people from God is not their strongholds - their unhealed hurts. The Bible makes clear that what separates people from God is their sin.

The seriousness of sin is illustrated by the fact that the Bible teaches that there was once a time when there was no death in the world. As seen above, death is a consequence of sin. I suspect that, to a large extent, problems in this area are caused by a failure to believe that the death brought into the world by Adam's sin was a real physical death.

Denis Alexander has, in recent years, become one of the foremost exponents of the idea that Adam's sin brought spiritual death. Dr Alexander is a professional scientist - a biologist at Cambridge University, and the

Director of the Faraday Institute - an association of names that could have the Bible-believing Michael Faraday spinning in his grave! Alexander, despite believing in the theory of evolution, argues strongly that Adam was a real person. In commenting on Romans 5, he says:

> There seems no reason to suppose that Paul doubted that the Adam of whom we spoke was a real person.[7]

His reasoning for this remarkable admission is that Paul uses Adam as a type of Jesus Christ. The parallel between Adam and Christ is seen in many places in the New Testament - most notably in Romans 5 and 1 Corinthians 15.

John Stott makes a similar point. In 1986, I had the privilege of hearing this great man deliver a lecture for the West Yorkshire School of Christian Studies, to coincide with the publication of his seminal work, *The Cross of Christ*. Stott strongly argued that the

---

[7] Alexander, D.R. (2008), *Creation or Evolution: Do we have to choose?*, (Oxford: Monarch), p265

aforementioned New Testament passages proved that one had to believe in a literal Adam. In the following question time, I was able to ask him about this, knowing that he believed in evolution. I asked what sort of person this Adam was, if he had descended from ape-like stock that lived and died like animals today. He argued that Adam's death at the Fall was spiritual. Moreover, he argued that Adam had been the first evolved ape-man, which is what was meant by Adam being formed from the dust of the earth, and that God breathed into him, so that he became *homo divinus*. Stott expanded on this point in his book, *Understanding the Bible*.

> My acceptance of Adam and Eve as historical is not incompatible with my belief that several forms of pre-Adamic 'hominid' may have existed for thousands of years previously. These hominids began to advance culturally. They made their cave drawings and buried their dead. It is conceivable that God created Adam out of one of them. You may call them homo erectus. I think you may even call some of them homo sapiens, for these are arbitrary scientific names. But Adam was the first

homo divinus, if I may coin a phrase, the first man to whom may be given the Biblical designation 'made in the image of God'. Precisely what the divine likeness was, which was stamped upon him, we do not know, for Scripture nowhere tells us. But Scripture seems to suggest that it includes rational, moral, social, and spiritual faculties which make man unlike all other creatures and like God the creator, and on account of which he was given 'dominion' over the lower creation.[8]

It should be noted that there are other theistic evolutionists who disagree with the *homo divinus* concept, beloved of Stott and Alexander. Others see Adam as a myth, rather than a historical reality. Michael Dowd comments:

Understanding the unwanted drives within us as having served our ancestors for millions of years is far more empowering than imagining that we are the way we are because of inner demons, or because the world's first woman and man ate a forbidden apple a few thousand years ago.[9]

[8] Stott, J.R.W., *Understanding the Bible*, p54-56

[9] Dowd, M. (2007), *Thank God for Evolution*, (San Francisco: Council Oak

Nevertheless, it is likely that the Stott/Alexander view of *homo divinus* is likely to be more appealing to those who claim to be Bible-believing evangelicals, so within their framework, we need to determine their definition of death.

Alexander bases his belief that Adam's sin brought *spiritual* death, rather than *physical* death, on God's warning to Adam in Genesis 2.

> Of the tree of the knowledge of good and evil you shall not eat, for **in the day that you eat of it you shall surely die.** (Genesis 2:17, emphasis mine)

Alexander compares this verse's use of the word day (Hebrew *yom*) with the word die. He claims that this verse underlines his figurative use of the word day in Genesis 1, and, therefore, also allows for a figurative interpretation of the word die.

> Just as Genesis 2:4 makes it very difficult to interpret *yom* as necessarily meaning a ay of 24 hours in the Genesis context, so equally the failure of Adam and Eve to physically drop dead on the

Books), p148

yom that they disobeyed God highlights once again the need to interpret the meanings of words by their context.[10]

Yet Alexander's error is precisely the failure to use the context. To discuss the use of the word *yom* would be a bunny trail at this point. Suffice to say that the word *yom* does not necessarily mean a 24-hour day, but it **always** means a 24-hour day when used in conjunction with a number.[11] On the subject of death, however, commentators have not in the past suggested that Adam should have dropped dead immediately. John Bunyan, the author of *Pilgrim's Progress*, said this in his fascinating commentary on Genesis:

> Adam lived to God no longer than while he kept himself from eating forbidden fruit; in that very day he died; first a spiritual death in his soul; his body also was then made capable of mortality, and

---

[10] Reference 7, p261

[11] For a detailed discussion of this point, please see Ham, K. *Could God Really Have Created Everything in Six Days?* In Ham, K. (ed.) (2006), *The New Answers Book 1*, (Green Forest, AR: Master Books), pp88-112

all diseases, which two great impediments in time brought him down to dust again.[12]

Calvin makes the same point.

> Wherefore the question is superfluous, how it was that God threatened death to Adam on the day in which he should touch the fruit, when he long deferred the punishment? For then was Adam consigned to death, and death began its reign in him, until supervening grace should bring a remedy.[13]

The key to understanding Genesis 2:17 is to look at the phrase **surely die**. The word *surely* is added for emphasis in the English. The Hebrew just has the word die - but uses the word twice. It is as if the verse is written "in the day that you eat of it you shall die die". I discussed this point in my book, *The Six Days of Genesis*.

> The Hebrew is die-die (תומת מות), which is often translated as "surely die" or literally as "dying you

---

[12] Bunyan, J. (edition 2010), *Genesis: A Commentary*, (Leicestershire: Just Six Days Publications), p55

[13] Calvin, G. (edition 1965), *A Commentary on Genesis*, (Edinburgh: Banner of Truth), pp127-128

shall die", which indicates the beginning of dying, an ingressive sense. At that point, Adam and Eve began to die and would return to dust. If they were meant to die right then, they would have used תומ only once as is used in the Hebrew meaning dead, died or die, and not *beginning to* die or *surely* die as die-die is used in Hebrew. From that point on, his physical death was inevitable. The fact that he lived another 930 years is irrelevant. If he had not sinned, he would still have been alive today and would have gone on living forever. In dying, he died.[14]

David Anderson, in his book *Creation or Evolution: Why we must choose*, has directly tackled Alexander's view about *spiritual* death being the punishment for Adam's disobedience.

> Dr Alexander ends up with the answer that the reason for physical death is that it is necessary for us to inherit the kingdom of God via the resurrection bodies, which could not have been done otherwise - though Dr Alexander then grants

---

[14] Taylor, P.F. (2007), *The Six Days of Genesis*, (Green Forest, AR: Master Books), p92

that in fact this is not necessary because those who are alive when Jesus returns *will* inherit the kingdom without physical death.... This leaves me wondering what Dr Alexander suppose would have happened to Adam if he had passed the test of the tree, and been admitted into life - would God have killed him anyway so that he could then have been resurrected?[15]

The idea of Adam's sin leading to a mere *spiritual* death, without *physical* death, does not stand up to biblical scrutiny. Moreover, it negates our entire hope for the future.

Dr Alexander... Concedes that the future kingdom of God will be without pain or suffering - because then it seems that God *could* in fact do such a thing... But Dr Alexander either never realizes, or simply decides to pretend not to notice, this glaring contradiction.[16]

[15] Anderson, D. (2009), *Creation or Evolution: Why we must choose*, (Leicestershire: Just Six Days Publications), p110

[16] Reference 15, p114

The issue of death in the future is of great importance to this issue. In Revelation, we read that in the New World to come, there will be "no more death" (Revelation 21:4), and that there will be "no more curse" (Revelation 22:3). These two statements immediately take us back to Genesis 3. If Adam's sin only brought in *spiritual* death - if *physical* death already existed in the world, then what sort of life in the world to come do we expect? Surely we cannot expect the end of *physical* death, because *physical* death was not associated with sin, according to the theistic evolutionists. Then the New World to come can only comprise of an everlasting *spiritual* life. Yet the language of Revelation suggests that this life has to be *physical*. George Eldon Ladd commented on the importance of the reality of the total and utter end of death.

> John means to affirm the final and complete destruction of death and the grave. It is true that Christ has "abolished", i.e. Broken the power of death by his own death and resurrection (II Timothy 1:10); but the saints still die. All that

eternal life means cannot be experienced until death itself is banished from the universe.[17]

Coming from a different eschatology, but equally committed to the truth of Revelation, creationist writer Dr Henry Morris said this about Revelation 22:3.

The agelong curse is gone. There is no more death and no more sin. The earth and its inhabitants, indeed the entire creation, are henceforth to thrive in fullest vigor forever. None will ever age, nothing will ever be lost, all work will be productive and enduring. The entropy law, the so-called second law of thermodynamics, will be repealed. Information will nevermore become confused, ordered systems will not deteriorate into disorder, and no longer will energy have to be expended merely to overcome friction and dissipation into nonrecoverable heat.[18]

[17] Ladd, G.E. (1972), *A Commentary on the Revelation of John*, (Grand Rapids, MI: Eerdmans), p274

[18] Morris, H.M. (1983), *The Revelation Record*, (Wheaton, IL: Tyndale House), p467

David Anderson has put hit the nail on the head, in the section quoted earlier, as far as the problematic theology of theistic evolution goes. The theistic evolutionist does not have a realistic theology of the future. At least the atheist evolutionist has a consistent eschatology! There has always been death in the past, there is death in the present, so there will always be death in the future. There is no future New Heaven and Earth to look forward to. One would have thought that theistic evolutionists would want to be inconsistent on these matters. Surely they would want to believe in the New Heaven and New Earth described in the Bible. Yet it seems this is not the case. Consider the consistency of these quotes from Alexander.

> Biological evolution is a slow process taking place over many millions, in fact billions of years.... The best current estimate for the age of the material which forms the earth is 4,566 million years. The universe is three times older, at 13,700 million years. Many people wonder how scientists can arrive at such dates, given the huge time-spans involved. Fortunately there are now many

different methods that can be used to arrive at essentially the same result.[19,20]

It is important to remember that the solar system was formed from a massive collision of material derived from meteorites which collected into discrete planetary bodies, including our own planet earth.[21]

The physical properties of the universe were defined in the very first few femtoseconds after the Big Bang, and the process of evolution depends utterly on that particular set of properties. Without them we would not be here.[22]

---

[19] Reference 7, p49

[20] Note how Alexander says that "different methods" give "**essentially** the same result" (emphasis mine). They do not give the same results. For a discussion of these different methods, and how different their results are, please see Vardiman, L. et al (eds.) (2000), *Radioisotopes and the Age of the Earth, Volume 1*, (El Cajon, CA: Institute for Creation Research). The key word is "essentially". This is code for saying that different methods do not actually give the same results, but they are "out" by fairly standard factors, so can be harmonised to give the same results, if the methods' presuppositions are changed.

[21] Reference 7, p51

[22] Reference 7, p135

One of the predictions for the final state of the
universe is a 'heat death' in which the second law
of thermodynamics will have the final word and
all matter will become further and further apart
and disorganized until entropy has increased to a
maximum extent.[23]

Readers should note Alexander's eschatology in the
final quote. It is completely in line with his notion of
billions of years of slow, evolutionary development.
He expects the same to go on for billions of years.
There is little here in the way of hope for the future.
Note the sort of language that Alexander uses, when
he does actually refer to the future, in his discussion of
the 'second death', mentioned in Revelation.

The actual phrase 'second death' appears only in
the book of Revelation, where it occurs four times.
The early suffering churches in Asia Minor are
reassured by the words of Jesus: 'He who has an
ear, let him hear what the Spirit says to the
churches. He who overcomes will not be hurt at all
by the second death' (Revelation 2:11). Then

---

[23] Reference 7, p139

finally (in Revelation 20:14) we learn that death itself is 'thrown into the lake of fire. The lake of fire is the second death'. **The Grim Reaper itself is ushered out of the drama even as the new heavens and the new earth are ushered in.**[24]

Remarkably, in the above quote, Alexander chooses to refer to death my what I assume he thinks is an amusing reference to a pagan symbolism of death. Now I am not opposed to humor - nor even to black humor. The implication of Alexander's use of language is that he seems to believe that this episode, like the early chapters of Genesis, are to be treated symbolically, rather than literally. Perhaps I am doing him an injustice, but it seems as if he does not believe that the New Heavens and New Earth will happen in the way that the Bible says they will. Perhaps he postpones this event in his mind billions upon billions of years hence, after the supposed heat death predicted by the Big Bang theory. In any event, his attitude provides no real substantial hope for the future. I have to say that, in the opinion of this author,

---

[24] Reference 7, pp252-253, emphasis mine

he has been helped by the prevailing eschatology of conservative evangelicals in the UK - including many of those who would agree with a literal reading of Genesis - who take a symbolic amillennial view of the future. It is worth noting that amillennialism is not the prevailing view among conservative evangelicals in the United States of America, where a different forms of premillennialism usually hold forth.

So the theistic evolutionists seem to have a very weak, sometimes symbolic view of death. They do not see death as an enemy, finally and literally defeated by Jesus' work on the cross. They may use the right words, when they discuss the cross of Jesus, but the weakness of their position on sin and death is seen in the context of their views on the whole of history - millions of years of death in the past, leading to millions of years of death into the future.

Other commentators have wanted strongly to emphasize the link between sin and death, and, therefore, the necessity of understanding that there was no death before Adam's sin. Wayne Grudem, despite taking an unfortunate old-earth position, states, in his *Systematic Theology*:

> It is important to insist on the historical truthfulness of the narrative of the fall of Adam and Eve. Just as the account of the creation of Adam and Eve is tied in with the r est of the historical narrative in the book of Genesis, so also this account of the fall of man, which follows the history of man's creation, is presented by the author as straightforward, narrative history. Moreover, the New Testament authors look back on this account and affirm that "sin came into the world through one man" (Romans 5:12) and insist that "the judgment following one trespass brought condemnation" (Romans 5:16) and that "the serpent deceived Eve by his cunning" (2 Corinthians 11:3; cf. 1 Timothy 2:14).[25]

In an important footnote to his text, Grudem shows how death is the punishment for sin, and how death happened for Adam and Eve.

---

[25] Grudem, W. (1994), *Systematic Theology*, (Leicester: Inter-Varsity Press), p493

The punishment of death began to be carried out on the day that Adam and Eve sinned, but it was carried out slowly over time, as their bodies grew old and they eventually died. The promise of spiritual death was put into effect immediately, since they were cut off from fellowship with God. The death of eternal condemnation was rightfully theirs, but the hints of redemption in the text (see Genesis 3:15, 21) suggest that this penalty was ultimately overcome by the redemption that Christ purchased.[26]

The Beginning of Sin and Death

With the bulk of the argument now rehearsed as a sort-of very lengthy introduction, we can now turn to the relevant section of Genesis 3 and see what the Bible describes as the origin of sin and death, having established that this is a historical narrative of an actual event. In case one final witness needed to be called, I will turn, in preparation to the words of one Martyn Lloyd-Jones - perhaps the greatest expository preacher of the 20th Century, and a man who is claimed, extraordinarily, as an influence by many

---

[26] Reference 25, p516

theistic evolutionists today. Some of Lloyd-Jones's sermons on Genesis have recently been gathered together in a wonderful little book, under the title *The Gospel in Genesis*, because Lloyd-Jones saw a belief in the literal truth of Genesis as essential to a proper understanding of the Gospel.

> Here is the most important key to history that is available at this moment. It explains the past. It explains the present. It explains the future. Let me put it as plainly as this: this is not allegory. I have no gospel unless this is history.[27]

Some of our discussion on the meaning of death in Genesis 3 we have already had in chapter 3 on the Inerrancy of Scripture. However, it is worth looking at how Genesis 3 should be expounded from verse 6 onwards, to see how the link between sin and death is so significant for the whole world.

> So when the woman saw that the tree was **good for food,** that it was **pleasant to the eyes,** and a tree **desirable** to make one wise, she took of its fruit

[27] Lloyd-Jones, D.M. (2009), *The Gospel in Genesis*, (Leominster: Day One Publications), p66

and ate. She also gave to her husband with her, and he ate. (Genesis 3:6, emphasis mine)

The emphasized phrases are words of temptation. They are words that appeal to the senses or the desires. They are not words that emphasize obedience. Consequently, we see that Eve has listened to the tempting words of Satan and has decided to fulfil her feelings, rather than thinking clearly. Note that Adam was "with her" while she was deciding these things - it is even possible that Adam was with her throughout the entire temptation, without intervening. After all, we read in 1 Timothy 2:14

Adam was not deceived, but the woman being deceived, fell into transgression.

So Eve's sin was simply her own, and she would bear the consequences of that sin. We will return to that point in a moment. Adam's sin, however, was on behalf of the human race. In a sense, he could be said to be the originator of the entire DNA of the human race - because Eve was not separately created, but created from Adam's side. This is important. Adam was

Eve's federal head, as much as he is ours. If this were not so then we could not have a new representative on behalf of the whole human race - that is the Last Adam, Jesus Christ.

> Then the eyes of both of them were opened, and they knew that they were naked; and they sewed fig leaves together and made themselves coverings. (Genesis 3:7)

Having their eyes opened was not the beginning of knowledge - rather it was the end of innocence. Their nakedness was symbolic of their lack of sin. Now they could not bear nakedness, as it was inappropriate in this new world of sin. So they made clothes of fig leaves. This means that they were trying to cover their nakedness, and hence their shame and guilt, by their own efforts. This would not protect them from the holiness of God.

> And they heard the sound of the LORD God walking in the garden in the cool of the day, and Adam and his wife hid themselves from the presence of the LORD God among the trees of the garden. (Genesis 3:8)

If I might be allowed to speculate for a moment, may I ask how Adam and Eve heard "the sound of the LORD God walking"? I do not want to make a major theological point on this, and I could be wrong, but I will suggest that, if God is able to walk, then what Adam and Eve were experiencing is a theophany - a pre-incarnate appearance of Jesus Himself. The description of the time as the "cool of the day" suggests that this was God's regular habit at this time, and suggests a pleasantness about Adam and Eve's communion with God. That pleasantness of fellowship had come to an end, as their sin had separated them from God. This was, if you like, the moment of *spiritual* death. So *spiritual* death had occurred before God's pronouncement of the curse. Therefore, the curse, which we will examine shortly, must have brought in actual *physical* death.

> Then the LORD God called to Adam and said to him, "Where are you?" (Genesis 3:9)

Why does God ask questions? He is omniscient; He already knows the answer. If He knows the answer, then the question cannot be for His benefit, since He does not require the information that such a probing question would bring. So if the question is not for God's benefit, it must be for Adam's benefit. Knowing what Adam has done, God is giving Adam the opportunity to repent.

> So he said, "I heard Your voice in the garden, and I was afraid because I was naked; and I hid myself." And He said, "Who told you that you were naked? Have you eaten from the tree of which I commanded you that you should not eat?" Then the man said, "The woman whom You gave to be with me, she gave me of the tree, and I ate." (Genesis 3:10-12)

Adam does not repent straight away. I have suggested in my commentary on Genesis 4,[28] that Adam and Eve may have subsequently repented. Once again, I will not make a dogmatic statement on this, but Eve's naming of Cain suggests that she and her husband had become believers. However, that is later in the story.

---

[28] Reference 14

> And the LORD God said to the woman, "What is this you have done?" The woman said, "The serpent deceived me, and I ate." (Genesis 3:13)

In turning to the woman, God is not letting Adam off the hook. We will see that, because of the nature of the curse that God will place on the man. However, Eve's salvation is separate from Adam in that she needs her own repentance. We only need the one **Savior**, but we each need our own **salvation**. At this point, however, the woman does not yet repent.

> So the LORD God said to the serpent: "Because you have done this, You are cursed more than all cattle, And more than every beast of the field; On your belly you shall go, And you shall eat dust All the days of your life. And I will put enmity Between you and the woman, And between your seed and her Seed; He shall bruise your head, And you shall bruise His heel." (Genesis 3:14-15)

God does not ask Satan a question. God already knows the reasons for what has happened. His questions to Adam and Eve were in mercy, to give the opportunity to repent. Satan has no such opportunity to repent. There is no salvation for a fallen angel. They were all separately created. Satan was not a federal head of fallen angels. They all made their own decision, and the consequences are theirs. So God launched straight into the curse on Satan. There were to be symbolic outward appearances of the curse on serpents in general, to remind us of the curse. But the specific issue is that found in verse 15. God presents the glorious Gospel - and Adam and Eve hear it. That Gospel gives no hope to Satan, but every hope to Adam and Eve, and all their descendents. One day there was to be the seed of the woman - but the seed is always from the man. God promises that He will send one who has no earthly father, but does have an earthly mother, to bruise or crush Satan. In the process, this Savior will be bruised or crushed - but only His heel, which suggests that He will rise again. If I am right that this walking, talking God is the Second Person of the Trinity, then in this wonderful moment, He is promising that He Himself will be born of a virgin (no earthly father) and will destroy Satan by dying for Adam and Eve and their descendents.

> To the woman He said: "I will greatly multiply your sorrow and your conception; In pain you shall bring forth children; Your desire shall be for your husband, And he shall rule over you." (Genesis 3:16)

Now God turns back to the woman. Remember that her sin was hers alone. So the curse on her is for her only - and possibly for women in general. But it is not a general curse on humanity. That is the curse for Adam, because he represented all of us.

> Then to Adam He said, "Because you have heeded the voice of your wife, and have eaten from the tree of which I commanded you, saying, 'You shall not eat of it': "Cursed is the ground for your sake; In toil you shall eat of it All the days of your life. Both thorns and thistles it shall bring forth for you, And you shall eat the herb of the field. In the sweat of your face you shall eat bread Till you return to the ground, For out of it you were taken; For dust you are, And to dust you shall return." And Adam called his wife's name Eve, because she was the mother of all living. (Genesis 3:17-20)

Although there are some startling effects that this curse was to have on Adam himself, we can see that the curse is more widespread. It affects Adam's descendents - all of us. And, more than that, it affects the whole of creation - "cursed is the ground for your sake". There is a major environmental change. Corruption and degradation is now the natural order. Work has become toil. And Adam is reminded that he will indeed return to the dust - the process of death has now begun, and will march to its inevitable conclusion.

So this passage makes clear that death - *physical* as well as *spiritual* - was not a part of God's creation. Death entered the universe because of Adam's sin. Death affects the entirety of creation. And death was to be personal, affecting Adam himself, as well as everything around him. Welcome to your new world, Adam. Welcome to a world in which there is no longer a close walk with God in the cool of the day, but a separation from Him, that will lead ever downwards to the grave.

> Also for Adam and his wife the LORD God made
> tunics of skin, and clothed them. (Genesis 3:21)

The use of the word "also" shows that this verse is also part of God's response to Adam's sin. And it is a response of mercy. Adam and Eve had tried to cover their guilt by their own efforts, in making clothes of fig leaves. Now God gives them clothes of skin - which requires the shedding of the blood of an animal. In a world, which had previously known no death, the first ever death was brought about by God Himself, in order to cover Adam and Eve's guilt. This is a glorious picture of the Gospel once again, which would find its fulfillment in the shedding of the blood of the Lamb of God, whose death would conquer death, and whose life would bring life, and in whom is the only hope we can or ought to have.

> So when this corruptible has put on incorruption,
> and this mortal has put on immortality, then shall
> be brought to pass the saying that is written:
> "DEATH IS SWALLOWED UP IN VICTORY. O DEATH,
> WHERE IS YOUR STING? O HADES, WHERE IS YOUR
> VICTORY?" The sting of death is sin, and the

strength of sin is the law. But thanks be to God, who gives us the victory through our Lord Jesus Christ. (1 Corinthians 15:54-57)

Doctrines of Salvation

Theistic evolutionists struggle with the deeper significant concepts behind the wonder of our salvation. How God has wrought things to bring us to salvation is an exciting topic - but the excitement is undermined, when so many of the essential prerequisites for our salvation are stated to be not quite true, but merely allegories, metaphors or literary devices.

Michael Dowd describes himself as a "full-time evolutionary evangelist".[1] He is the author of the book *Thank God for Evolution*. His claim that he loves evolution and the Bible appears to be only half right, as his view of salvation is somewhat unorthodox. His invented word, *creatheism*, is explained after the discussion of this quote.

> From a creatheistic perspective, to think that "getting right" or "being right" with God requires one to hold a particular set of beliefs implies that God is beset with human limitations. If a person is

[1] Dowd, M. (2007), *Thank God for Evolution*, (San Francisco: Council Oak Books), pxxviii

expected to give mental assent to word-based propositions in order to be "saved", then God's love is hardly unconditional, nor is God's wisdom infinite. To interpret "faith in God" as meaning that one must subscribe to a particular way of seeing the world in order to go to an unnatural or otherworldly place called "heaven" is to miss out on the this-world saving grace of the Gospel. Those who cling to flat-earth theological positions on biblical grounds diss the Holy One. To imply that the best guidance for interpreting salvation or any other doctrine is to be found in 2000-year-old texts is to declare God as cruel, uncaring and impotent.[2]

Dowd's analysis is one of those examples where people use the same words as the Bible, but give them a totally different meaning. He talks about salvation, but has no concept of what we are to be saved from or saved to. He doesn't even believe in the reality of heaven, let alone the reality of hell - a place of punishment for those who have chosen to bear their own sins, and reap the consequences thereof. Where

---

[2] Reference 1, p182

Dowd makes his mistake is in assuming that biblical ideas of salvation come from within our thoughts. They do not. They come from God's ordering of things, as reported in the Bible. What he describes as "flat-earth" theological positions are therefore those which are grounded on a presupposition that scripture is true. His claim not to have a presupposition is false. His presupposition is that scripture is mythological and literary rather than actually true - but he gives no such qualifications to his interpretation of what he calls "science". It is his assumption that something which is 2000 years old is by definition in error. The Bible knows of no such limitation to its own effectiveness. The one who has the disrespect for God, therefore, is not the one who accepts scripture, since it is the word of God, but the one who rejects it - like Dowd himself.

By the way, his use of the invented term *creatheism* is an attempt to find some sort of common ground between theism and atheism - I kid you not!

Occasionally, someone who has heard me speak asks in frustration, "What *are* you, anyway? A theist? Atheist? Pantheist? I can't tell what you are!" My standard response goes something like this: "I'm all of those—and none of them. Actually, my wife and I had to coin our own term. I'm a creatheist (cree-uh-THEIST) and my wife, well, she's a creatheist (cree-ATHEIST). We spell it the same way. We mean the same thing. We just pronounce it differently." This response almost always evokes smiles or laughter.[3]

Not here it didn't! It just evoked weeping.

Clearly, there are other theistic evolutionists, whose traditions supposedly put them inside the evangelical camp. John Stott, for example, links the entire Bible with the doctrine of salvation.

> So the Bible is primarily a book neither of science, nor of literature, nor of philosophy, but of salvation. In saying this we must give the word 'salvation' its broadest possible meaning. Salvation is far more than merely the forgiveness of sins. It includes the whole sweep of God's purpose to redeem and restore humankind and indeed all

---

[3] Reference 1, p117

creation. What we claim for the Bible is that it unfolds God's total plan.[4]

None of us, who take a biblical Christian view, would differ with this analysis of the purpose of the Bible. However, Stott has emphasized that all creation is included in "the whole sweep of God's purpose to redeem". So his analysis comes unstuck at the first hurdle, as he loses his authority to back the above statement up.

> My acceptance of Adam and Eve as historical is not incompatible with my belief that several forms of pre-Adamic 'hominid' seem to have existed for thousands of years previously. These hominids began to advance culturally. They made their cave drawings and buried their dead. It is conceivable that God created Adam out of one of them.[5]

In which case, we are entitled to ask why God said that He had made Adam out of dust, rather than out of a pre-Adamic hominid. If these pre-Adamic people had

---

[4] Stott, J.(1972), *Understanding the Bible*, (Milton Keynes: Scripture Union), p4

[5] Reference 4, p43

culture, how could they not have souls? And what is the purpose of believing in the historicity of Adam - in order to accept the contrast illustrated in 1 Corinthians 15 - if the very reason for the contrast (Paul's argument about the introduction of sin into the world, causing death) is actually undermined by one's belief in human evolution?

Denis Alexander examines five number of possible models for interpreting the account of Adam and Eve. His "Model C", which he favors, is the one proposed by Stott, with pre-Adamic hominids, and human evolution, but a real historical Adam and Eve. He disingenuously points out the limitations of the model.

> Model C will not answer all the theological questions that one might like to ask. For example, what was the eternal destiny of all those who lived before Adam and Eve? The answer really is that we have no idea. But we can be assured with Abraham: "Will not the Judge of all the earth do right?" (Genesis 18:25)[6]

[6] Alexander, D. (2008), *Creation or Evolution: Do we have to choose?*, (Oxford: Monarch), p243

Alexander's twisting of scripture out of context masks the paucity of his theological position. What sort of a God condemns pre-Adamic people, complete with their culture, to death, when death is a result of sin? Admittedly, Alexander believes that Adam's death introduced spiritual death. But the mere introduction of spiritual death never explains why, in paying the penalty for our sins, the Last Adam had to die a real death, not just a spiritual death.

A book of this size cannot hope to cover in depth all the doctrines that could necessarily be included in a Systematic Theology. Nor can it cover any individual doctrine to the depth that it deserves. But this book is not a Systematic Theology. It is merely taking some example doctrines, and showing that they are built on a foundation best understood by taking the early chapters of Genesis as historical truth. In a Systematic Theology, the various doctrines concerning salvation, which are included in this chapter, would certainly have chapters of their own. The theological words that we will look at in this chapter are *atonement, grace, justification* and *sanctification*.

It has often been said that scientists use big words so that they can appear smart.[7] Perhaps the same can be said of theologians! Yet a technical word can sometimes be of help, as it directs our attention towards an important aspect of God's work. All that is necessary is for the "big word" to be explained and then used accurately and consistently. The suspicion is that the afore-mentioned "clever people" are probably using big words to hide their own lack of understanding, or to shield from their listeners or readers that their arguments lack the coherence or articulation that is initially apparent. Our use of such technical terms should only be to clarify and simplify. It is indeed possible for technical terms to be used in this latter sense. So, for the purposes of this chapter, I will define the terms, look at the doctrines in the New Testament, then the Old Testament, and finally their foundation in Genesis.

---

[7] I found this comment recently in a Facebook discussion!

Definitions

Atonement

There are frivolous definitions for a couple of these terms, usually based on coincidences of the English language. In the case of *atonement*, therefore, some have suggested that it means "at-one-ment" - i.e. being at one with God. The trouble with the frivolous definitions is that they usually contain *part* of the truth, but don't give a full explanation. Being "at one" with God is part of the outworking of the atonement, but doesn't begin to cover the whole range of meanings of this beautiful word - the principle meaning of which is "cover".

A lot of what we understand by *atonement* is to be found in those boring parts of the Bible that we like to skip over - in Leviticus and Numbers. There was an important ritual involved in receiving atonement. Take, for example, the account of the Sin Offering in Leviticus 4.

> Now if the whole congregation of Israel sins unintentionally, and the thing is hidden from the

eyes of the assembly, and they have done something against any of the commandments of the LORD in anything which should not be done, and are guilty; when the sin which they have committed becomes known, then the assembly shall offer a young bull for the sin, and bring it before the tabernacle of meeting. And the elders of the congregation shall lay their hands on the head of the bull before the LORD. Then the bull shall be killed before the LORD. The anointed priest shall bring some of the bull's blood to the tabernacle of meeting. Then the priest shall dip his finger in the blood and sprinkle it seven times before the LORD, in front of the veil. And he shall put some of the blood on the horns of the altar which is before the LORD, which is in the tabernacle of meeting; and he shall pour the remaining blood at the base of the altar of burnt offering, which is at the door of the tabernacle of meeting. He shall take all the fat from it and burn it on the altar. And he shall do with the bull as he did with the bull as a sin offering; thus he shall do with it. So the priest shall make atonement for them, and it shall be forgiven them. Then he shall carry the bull outside the camp, and burn it as he burned the first bull. It is a sin offering for the assembly. (Leviticus 4:13-21)

Before the sacrifice of the bull, there was a confession of sins. Following this confession, the bull was killed, and then blood was sprinkled in an important ritual. By so doing, the priest was making atonement for them. Thus, the atonement covered sin by the shedding of blood.

The regulations for the Day of Atonement (*Yom Kippur*) are even more striking. The account of the Day of Atonement is found in Leviticus 16. Arnold Fruchtenbaum has shown that the details of the Day of Atonement can be divided into seven segments.[8] To begin with, there were extensive preparations for the sacrifice, to make sure it was done correctly. Because the priest is himself a human, with human failings and sins, he first had to offer a sacrifice for his own sins. Then he was able to offer a sacrifice for the sins of the people. After this, all the participants were cleansed and set apart. The following chapter offers this

[8] Fruchtenbaum, A. *Yom Kippur - The Day of Atonement*, MBS119, from < www.ariel.org >, p12-17

remarkable insight into the importance of the Day of Atonement.

> For the life of the flesh is in the blood, and I have given it to you upon the altar to make atonement for your souls; for it is the blood that makes atonement for the soul. (Leviticus 17:11)

The first part of this verse refers back to Genesis 1. Certain creatures contain blood, and they are the ones which were blessed by God. The Hebrew word is *nephesh* (נפש), and in Genesis 1, it is translated either as *life* or as *creature*, illustrating that these are the animals with blood. Leviticus 17:11 says "the life of the flesh is in the blood", illustrating the great importance attached to blood, particularly in sacrifice. Leviticus 17:11 then goes on to state that the sacrifice of blood is "to make atonement for your **souls**" (emphasis mine). Our souls need a covering for sin. Obviously, they need more than a covering, because these sacrifices had to be repeated over and over again, whereas Jesus' sacrifice was once for all. Nevertheless, it is important that we understand the messianic significance of Leviticus 16.

Hebrews has much more to say on this subject. Hebrews emphasizes that Jesus fulfilled the requirements for priesthood, and therefore able to offer the sacrifices for sins. Jesus was of the tribe of Judah, rather than Levi, so it was also important to note that his priesthood was not of the order of Aaron, but of the earlier order of Mechizedek,[9] making his priesthood eternal rather than temporal. Hebrews then goes on to show that Jesus is not only the priest, but also the mediator of the covenant and himself the perfect object of sacrifice. In many ways, perhaps the most remarkable chapter of Hebrews dealing with this issue is Hebrews 9, especially from verse 16 onwards.

> For where there is a testament, there must also of necessity be the death of the testator. For a testament is in force after men are dead, since it has no power at all while the testator lives. Therefore not even the first covenant was dedicated without blood. For when Moses had spoken every precept to all the people according to the law, he took the blood of calves and goats,

---

[9] Hebrews 5.

with water, scarlet wool, and hyssop, and sprinkled both the book itself and all the people, saying, "This is the blood of the covenant which God has commanded you." Then likewise he sprinkled with blood both the tabernacle and all the vessels of the ministry. And according to the law almost all things are purified with blood, and without shedding of blood there is no remission. (Hebrews 9:16-22)

The sacrifices of atonement had to be repeated. Jesus' sacrifice was the fulfillment of all these Days of Atonement and other sacrifices. However, Jesus' death was a one-off sacrifice, which does not need to be repeated. The reason for this is seen further on in Hebrews 9.

Therefore it was necessary that the copies of the things in the heavens should be purified with these, but the heavenly things themselves with better sacrifices than these. For Christ has not entered the holy places made with hands, which are copies of the true, but into heaven itself, now to appear in the presence of God for us; not that He should offer Himself often, as the high priest enters the Most Holy Place every year with blood of another— He then would have had to suffer often since the foundation of the world; but now, once at the end of the ages, He has appeared to put away sin by the sacrifice of Himself. And as it is appointed for men to die once, but after this the judgment, so Christ was offered once to bear the sins of many. To those who eagerly wait for Him He will appear a second time, apart from sin, for salvation. (Hebrews 9:23-28)

This wonderful section of scripture shows that the sacrifices were only "copies of the things in the heavens", and reminds us that atoning sacrifices had to be repeated. Not so the ultimate sacrifice of the Son of God - our Savior and Messiah.

To emphasize this important point, the apostle John twice uses the word *propitiation* to describe what Jesus has done - a word that also occurs in Hebrews 2:17. The word *propitiation* means "the removal of wrath by the offering of a gift"[10].

---

[10] Illustrated Bible Dictionary (1980), (Leicester, IVP), p1287

> And He Himself is the propitiation for our sins, and not for ours only but also for the whole world. (1 John 2:2)

> In this is love, not that we loved God, but that He loved us and sent His Son to be the propitiation for our sins. (1 John 4:10)

Propitiation is a translation of the Greek word *hilasmos* (ἱλασμός). Some versions, notably the NIV, translate this as "atoning sacrifice". What we understand from this is that our sin causes God to be angry with our sin. However, Jesus' atoning sacrifice perfectly covers this sin, thus turning away the wrath of God. It must be mentioned that the RSV likes to translate *hilasmos* with the word *expiation*. The Illustrated Bible Dictionary says that this is because "Expiation properly has a thing as its object. We may expiate a crime or a sin.... We propitiate a person rather than a sin"[11]. The reason for this substitution is that some find it difficult to imagine God being angry with us, even though the Old Testament contains much on this subject.

[11] IBD, p491

The fact that Hebrews continually quotes from and comments on passages from Leviticus, and other pertinent parts of the Old Testament, shows that the arguments given in Hebrews are not a novel add-on to scripture. They are foreshadowed in messianic prophetic passages of the Old Testament Two of the most clear examples of this are in Isaiah 53 and in Psalm 22.

> Therefore I will divide Him a portion with the great, And He shall divide the spoil with the strong, Because He poured out His soul unto death, And He was numbered with the transgressors, And He bore the sin of many, And made intercession for the transgressors. (Isaiah 53:12)

This verse shows that the Messiah Himself is to be the sacrifice, as well as the priest. He offered Himself, and therefore bore the sin of many, in a manner which does not require repetition - indeed, such repetition would be impossible. It is also remarkable that the sacrificial manner of the death of the Messiah is also foretold in Psalm 22.

I am poured out like water, And all My bones are out of joint; My heart is like wax; It has melted within Me. My strength is dried up like a potsherd, And My tongue clings to My jaws; You have brought Me to the dust of death. (Psalm 22: 14-15)

Atonement may indeed involve being given "at-one-ment" with God, but it is the mechanism of preparation and covering with blood that is actually important for the salvation of our souls.

Grace

Like *atonement*, *grace* can also be given a frivolous meaning. There are some who define it as if it were an acronym - God's Riches At Christ's Expense. This definition also contains some of the truth, but the whole truth is so much greater.

Grace is basically synonymous with *favor*. It is perhaps easiest to define grace by looking at one of the most famous passages in the New Testament that uses the term - Ephesians 2:8-9.

For by grace you have been saved through faith, and that not of yourselves; it is the gift of God, not of works, lest anyone should boast.

This passage shows that we are saved by grace. This grace has come to us through faith. But even the faith itself has not come from ourselves. It is not a work - it is a gift. We cannot earn a gift, otherwise it would not be a gift. If we were able to get our salvation by anything that we do ourselves, then it would be an earned salvation. Almost every heretical or erroneous version of the gospel comes unstuck at this point, because it is only true faith in Jesus that brings salvation.

Perhaps we might ask someone to do us a favor. Maybe the other party asks for something in return. If they do, then it is not a favor - it is a deal or a bargain. A favor is something done or given, without the benefit of receiving anything in return. True grace, therefore, does not involve exchange. If we have received a favor, then we have nothing to boast about. Even the faith that we exercise, through which we obtain grace, has not come from ourselves. Even that faith is the gift of God.

Romans 6:23 gives us further insight into this matter.

> For the wages of sin is death, but the gift of God is eternal life in Christ Jesus our Lord.

Wages are what we earn. The only thing that we, as sinners, can possibly earn from God is death. We cannot earn eternal life, because that would require good work, but Paul has earlier in this letter emphasized that "All have sinned". (Romans 3:23) Therefore, the only way we can get eternal life is as a gift. And the only way that the gift of eternal life is possible is because of the propitiating work of Jesus Christ. Thus we see that the fact of the grace of God is inextricably linked to God's removal of our sin, through the work of His Son.

This understanding of the concept of grace has been a source of contention for centuries - indeed, it was this issue which was at the heart of the Reformation. Grudem states:

In distinction from the Roman Catholic teaching that we are justified by God's grace *plus some merit of our own*, as we make ourselves fit to receive the grace of justification and as we grow in this state of grace through our good works, Luther and the other Reformers insisted that justification comes by grace *alone*, not by grace plus some merit on our part.[12]

In the Old Testament, there are a couple of words which are sometimes translated as *grace*, but the main one of these is the word *hên* (), of which the Illustrated Bible Dictionary says:

This is not a covenant word and not two-way. It is used of the action of a superior, human or divine, to an inferior.

We see its use in Ruth's comment to Naomi.

So Ruth the Moabitess said to Naomi, "Please let me go to the field, and glean heads of grain after him in whose sight I may find favor." (Ruth 2:2)

---

[12] Grudem, W. (1994), *Systematic Theology*, (Leicester: IVP), p729, emphases his

We see the use of this word in the context of God's grace in Jeremiah 31:2.

> Thus says the LORD: "The people who survived the sword found grace in the wilderness—Israel, when I went to give him rest."

Both New Testament and Old Testament agree that grace is one-way - an unmerited favor, that cannot be returned or earned..

Justification

The third of the four doctrines of salvation that we are looking at (out of the several that we could have chosen) also has a trivial definition. It has been suggested that we are justified from our sins, so it is therefore "just as if" we had never sinned.

The real significance of the term *justification* is that it is a legal term. The Hebrew word is *sadaq* (צְדַק) and the Greek word is *dikaioō* (δικαιόω). In both cases, the implication is of someone appearing before a judge, and being acquitted of a crime.

If there is a dispute between men, and they come to court, that the judges may judge them, and they justify the righteous and condemn the wicked, then it shall be, if the wicked man deserves to be beaten, that the judge will cause him to lie down and be beaten in his presence, according to his guilt, with a certain number of blows. (Deuteronomy 25:1-2)

He who justifies the wicked, and he who condemns the just, Both of them alike are an abomination to the LORD. (Proverbs 17:15)

Who shall bring a charge against God's elect? It is God who justifies. (Romans 8:33)

The passages in the Old Testament which use *sadaq* are translated *dikaioō* in the Septuagint (which is the early translation of the Old Testament into Greek), emphasizing the equivalence of these terms. This legal definition of justification - being made righteous - is seen clearly in the change of status of a repentant believer. The passage above from Proverbs shows that it is an abomination simply to declare a wicked person to be righteous, without any grounds for doing so.

Therefore, the only grounds on which God declares sinners righteous is through the merits and work of Jesus Christ. It is His sacrifice which propitiates the wrath of God and enables God to declare us righteous - i.e. to justify us.

> But to him who does not work but believes on Him who justifies the ungodly, his faith is accounted for righteousness. (Romans 4:5)

This concept of justification is therefore so clearly linked with the concept of atonement, and also of grace. How can the ungodly be justified? Only by faith - and that faith, we have learned, comes only by grace. The concept of justification can only be found in its fulfillment in the New Testament. Its use in the Old Testament is to show its impossibility, and it is only possible because of Jesus. Nevertheless, we get a hint about its coming, in Messianic passages, such as Psalm 32.

> Blessed is he whose transgression is forgiven, Whose sin is covered. Blessed is the man to whom

> the LORD does not impute iniquity, And in whose
> spirit there is no deceit. (Psalm 32:1-2)

So, in this particular case, the trivial definition actually works. The Christian has sinned, and deserves wrath. But, because the punishment has already been made (on the cross), the sinner can be declared righteous - so it really is just as if he had never sinned!

Sanctification

Grudem defines sanctification as "a progressive work of God and man that makes us more and more free from sin and like Christ in our actual lives."[13] Grudem also helpfully includes a table (below), which shows the differences between sanctification and justification.

In a sense, we should emphasize that sanctification is not to do with our ultimate salvation. Sanctification is about our improvement, by our good works. Our good works, however, do not save us. Nevertheless, there is a link with our salvation, in that it is assumed

---

[13] Grudem, W. (1994), p746

Justification	Sanctification
Legal standing	Internal condition
Once for all time	Continuous throughout life
Entirely God's work	We cooperate
Perfect in this life	Not perfect in this life
The same in all Christians	Greater in some than in others

that our sanctification has a definite beginning at our salvation.

> But you were washed, but you were sanctified, but you were justified in the name of the Lord Jesus and by the Spirit of our God. (1 Corinthians 6:11)

The use of the past tense, in this passage, suggests it is something that has happened. Yet we also know that it is an ongoing process, so 1 Corinthians 6 must be referring to its beginning. The New Testament also shows us that this act of one being made holy - which is what sanctification means - is an indication that the Christian has been saved, and the lack of sanctification is an indication that salvation is not really present.

This is how most commentators interpret the discussion about faith and works in James 2:14-26. This is how one study Bible footnotes the passage in James.

> James does not set faith against works, but rather discusses two kinds of faith: a dead faith and a saving faith. Saving faith is not simply a profession or an empty claim, nor is it merely the acceptance of a creed. Saving faith is that which produces an obedient life. Paul's emphasis on the Christian life at its inception (justification) is not antagonistic to James's position, for Paul, too, believes in justification producing the fruit of works (Galatians 5:6).[14]

Although this necessity of holy living is expounded most fully in the New Testament, the Old Testament is not without the concept.

> For I am the LORD your God. You shall therefore consecrate yourselves, and you shall be holy; for I am holy. (Leviticus 11:44)

---

[14] Hayford, J. (ed.) (2002), *The Spirit-Filled Life Bible*, (Nashville, TN: Thomas Nelson), p1794, footnote to James 2:14-26.

In many cases, the concept of holiness or sanctification in the Old Testament seems to refer simply to a ceremonial setting apart, in other passages, such as this from Leviticus, an aspect of behavior also appears to be present.

Foundation in Genesis

The four aspects of salvation that we have chosen can all be seen reflected in Genesis, to a greater or lesser extent.

The actual word *sanctified* only occurs in Genesis in reference to God setting apart the seventh day as the Sabbath.

> Then God blessed the seventh day and sanctified it, because in it He rested from all His work which God had created and made. (Genesis 2:3)

Nevertheless, the concept of sanctification - in our behavior and striving to be holy - does appear founded in Genesis. In the sanctification of the seventh day, God was setting a pattern for us to follow. This is seen further in the restatement of the principle as part of the Ten Commandments in Exodus 20.

Remember the Sabbath day, to keep it holy. Six days you shall labor and do all your work, but the seventh day is the Sabbath of the LORD your God. In it you shall do no work: you, nor your son, nor your daughter, nor your male servant, nor your female servant, nor your cattle, nor your stranger who is within your gates. For in six days the LORD made the heavens and the earth, the sea, and all that is in them, and rested the seventh day. Therefore the LORD blessed the Sabbath day and hallowed it. (Exodus 20:8-11)

It is noteworthy that this, the Fourth Commandment, is the only one where a reason is given, and that reason harks straight back to Genesis. Since the sanctification of the Sabbath is a creation ordinance, there is no suggestion that its sanctification no longer applies. In dealing with this subject, Andy McIntosh first shows how the New Testament record clearly shifted the day of the Sabbath from the seventh to the first day. He then comments on the lack of observance of the Lord's Day in today's society:

The church by and large has conceded this day, by not keeping it. Because she had not kept the day, she has lost the privilege and has also caused incalculable damage to the cause of the gospel in England and many Western nations. The church itself is now today far weaker as a result.[15]

The issue of the right behavior of God's people is reflected in God's injunction on Cain, that he should resist sin.

So the LORD said to Cain, "Why are you angry? And why has your countenance fallen? If you do well, will you not be accepted? And if you do not do well, sin lies at the door. And its desire is for you, but you should rule over it." (Genesis 4:6)

A life of sin is the opposite of what the followers of God should be doing. Of course, this is outside of Cain's experience, as his subsequent actions show. As I have written in my book *Cain and Abel*, Cain really has no understanding of his actual state before God, nor of his need for salvation.[16]

---

[15] McIntosh, A. (2006, 3rd edition), *Genesis for Today*, (Leominster: Day One Publications), p97

The concept of *justification* is most clearly seen in Genesis in the life of Abraham. The following event in the life of Abraham is so important to an understanding of justification that it is quoted more than in the New Testament.

In Genesis 15, God emphasizes to Abraham (or Abram, as he was called at that time) that his heir would be "from your own body".

> Then He brought him outside and said, "Look now toward heaven, and count the stars if you are able to number them." And He said to him, "So shall your descendants be." (Genesis 15:5).

This was an important restatement and clarification of the promise given previously to Abraham, at a time when such fulfillment of the promise seemed more humanly possible (Genesis 12). In another chapter of this book, I have emphasized that neither Abraham nor Sarah were too old to bear children at the time of leaving Haran, but by the events of Genesis 15, Sarah had certainly become too old. Although Sarah was 65

[16] Taylor, P. *Cain and Abel: Worship and Sacrifice*, (Leicestershire: Just Six Days Publications)

when they left Haran, this was proportionately equivalent to a modern age of thirty-something, bearing in mind the longer age-span enjoyed by Abraham and Sarah. However, despite not being too old to bear children when they left Haran, Sarah could not bear children, because the Bible makes it clear that she was barren - with all the shame that this condition would bring in such society. Into this seemingly impossible situation, God brings His promise to Abraham that he will indeed have a son, and this son will be an heir of his own flesh, with numerous descendents. Abraham's reaction takes just one sentence, but its implications have thundered down the millennia since.

> And he believed in the LORD, and He accounted it
> to him for righteousness. (Genesis 15:6)

Abraham was a sinner, like any other man. In Genesis 12:1`0-20 - early in our reading of the history of Abraham - he had let God down badly by his lack of faith and lack of principle in Egypt. As a descendent of Adam, Abraham started with a negative credit sheet - a huge debt against his name, from his sin and disobedience. So Genesis 15:6 is of enormous significance. What did Abraham do? Nothing, in the sense of action. He simply believed God. He had faith. God had given a promise, and Abraham had to come to accept the fact that God is completely trustworthy. So Abraham knew that what God had promised would definitely happen, despite the seemingly impossible nature of it all. God is all-powerful. What God has said WILL happen. And it is that faith of Abraham which was his salvation. Not only was Abraham saved by faith, but God justified Abraham. Abraham's debt sheet now had a huge credit, which overwrote the debt of sin. "He [God] accounted it to him for righteousness." Abraham had been justified - it was just as if he had never sinned, to use our trivial definition! Abraham still failed and still sinned. In Genesis 16, Abraham and Sarah tried to fulfil God's promise by their own methods, and so Ishmael was born. And in Genesis 20, Abraham repeats his error from his time in Egypt by his attitudes in the kingdom of Abimelech. Yet we will encounter Abraham in heaven. Why? Because he was justified by his faith.

Abraham believed - and God credited it to him as righteousness.

The concept of *atonement* seems to appear first in Genesis 3. What clothes did Adam and Eve wear? Most people picture them in fig leaves - yet they did not wear fig leaves very long. They wore fig leaves, because of their guilt and nakedness. They were trying to cover their guilt by their own methods. Yet we can never cover our own guilt. The word *atonement*, which in Hebrew comes from the root *kâphar* (Strong's number H3722 - .כפֵּר), means *covering*. After God had pronounced the curse in Genesis 3, and had given the first revelation of the Gospel in Genesis 3:15, we read that "for Adam and his wife the LORD God made tunics of skin, and clothed them." (Genesis 3:21). In a perfect world, in which there was no death, but into which sin had now come, God caused the first ever death of an animal in order to provide skins to clothe Adam and Eve - to *cover* them; to *atone* for their sins. We cannot cover our own guilt with fig leaves. We need the shedding of blood to atone for our sins.

The interesting occurrence of the Hebrew *kâphar* is in Genesis 6. It would be easy to miss it - yet the word appears twice in Genesis 6:14.

Make yourself an ark of gopherwood; make rooms in the ark, and cover it inside and outside with pitch.

The usage is easy to miss, as two English words are used. The two words concerned are *cover* and *pitch.* Pitch is a waterproof covering. Today, it would usually be made out of heavy petroleum fractions, and this has caused hang-ups for many people, as many creationists have supposed that petroleum would have been formed organically during the Flood, and would therefore not have been available before the Flood. However, prior to the rise of petroleum industries, pitch was manufactured from other sources, such as the tar left behind from hearing wood. In any case, Genesis 6 is not concerned with the actual source of the pitch - merely that a covering substance was clearly used to waterproof the Ark. However, the significance of this has theological implications. The Ark is a *type* of Christ. Jesus is our ark of salvation.

Pitch waterproofed the Ark against the watery judgment of God. The atoning sacrifice of Jesus fireproofs us against the judgment of God to come.

Finally, for this section, we turn our attention to the use of the concept of *grace* in Genesis. This is the clearest of our doctrines of salvation to see in Genesis. We also find this word in Genesis 6. It is there in God's reason for saving Noah from the Flood.

> Noah found grace in the eyes of the LORD. (Genesis 6:8)

Noah was not saved because of his personal righteousness - after all, we find that after the Flood he made his own mistakes, such as getting drunk. The righteousness that Noah had was not from himself. Hebrews 11 tells us where his righteousness came from.

> By faith Noah, being divinely warned of things not yet seen, moved with godly fear, prepared an ark for the saving of his household, by which he condemned the world and became heir of the righteousness which is according to faith. (Hebrews 11:7)

Noah's righteousness was "according to faith". And his faith, according to Genesis 6:8, came from grace. Noah was saved by grace through faith. Where did we read that before?

> For by **grace** you have been saved through **faith**, and that not of yourselves; it is the gift of God, not of works, lest anyone should boast. (Ephesians 2:8-9 - emphasis mine)

Not only does Genesis 6:8 remind us of how Noah was saved, it also remind us that the method of salvation has always been the same. Just as we read the first account of the Gospel immediately after the first sin (Genesis 3:15), so our response to that Gospel has always been the same - repentance and faith, with salvation by the grace of God. Therefore, the only difference in the mode of salvation between Old and New Testaments is that, in the Old, they were looking ahead to the Messiah to come, whereas in the New, we look back to the Messiah who has been and has died for our sins.

Abraham in Context

The New Testament looks back to Abraham as our supreme example of faith. Quite rightly, a lot of commentators have made much of this issue. It matters to them that Abraham was a real person in history, so that they can trace the development of genuine faith back to him. But the life of Abraham starts in Genesis 12 – well, there is a little bit about him at the end of Genesis 11, actually. This causes a problem to those people who want to hold to an evangelical theology of the Bible, but who do not want to accept the first eleven chapters of Genesis as literally true. It is the case, after all, that the histories recorded in Genesis 12 to 50 are in the same style as the histories recorded in Genesis 1 to 11. Genesis 1 to 11 is not part of a separate book. The book of beginnings is one book, written in one style.

The fact that the first mentions of Abraham (or Abram as he then was, so that is the name we ought to use from now on) are in Genesis 11 is problematic. It would be nice for some to be able to dismiss the first eleven chapters completely, but, if they did that, they would lose the references to Abram.

When we dig a bit deeper, we find something interesting. Simply trying to begin the account of Abram in Genesis 12, without referring back to the first eleven chapters, leads to a skewed and problematic view of his amazing life. However, if we start by believing the account of Genesis 1 to 11 as factual history, a number of facts about Abram's life suddenly fall into place, and become easier to explain and understand.

Abram's Genealogy

Don't you find the genealogies boring? It's so tedious, isn't it, to keep reading that so-and-so begat so-and-so and so on. Yet it seems to be a given that God did not put anything in the Bible which wasn't supposed to be there. So how do we understand what is being meant by the genealogies of Genesis 5 and 11?

Several reasons have been put forward, even by Young Earth Creationists, as to why these genealogies should contain gaps. Some of this has been due to embarrassment over archaeological dates of Egypt and Babylon. Yet this acceptance of modern dating methods is precisely what Young Earth Creationists oppose in other aspects of their arguments. In the opinion of this writer, the problem is that many Young Earth Creationists have taken their position of the Earth being under 10,000 years old from the failure of dating methods – a negative argument – rather than using the positive argument of simply accepting the timescales in the Bible. In other words, their rejection of old earth chronology has not started with a presupposition of scriptural accuracy, a point which I have made in the past[1,2]. Dr. Monty White has argued that any gaps there might be in the genealogies of Genesis 5 and 11 cannot be great. White says:

> Although we do not know for certain whether there are any gaps in the genealogies in Genesis 5 and 11, we can be certain that, if there are any, they are not huge. We can be confident, therefore, that although we may not be able to date the

[1] Bush, A., Flood models and chronogenealogy, *TJ* **18**(1):62–63, 2004

[2] Taylor, P., Flood boundary debate, *TJ* **18**(1):62, 2004

creation of Adam exactly, it is doubtful whether it could have been much earlier than 4004 BC.[3]

While he has arrived at an acceptable final answer, it has to be said that Dr White's comment has completely missed the point. It is not for us to pass judgment on the book of Genesis, and decide whether or not the genealogical gaps are great or not. Rather, we start from scripture, assume that it means what it says, and work accordingly.

Larry Pierce and Ken Ham have made clear that they do not accept White's concept of minor gaps. Their article on the subject – published in the New Answers Book 2 – does not allow for such gaps.

> Genesis 11... features 10 generations over 355 years, therefore averaging 36 years per generation. Those who hold to a creation occurring in 10,000 B.C. and the Flood happening in 5,000 B.C. have expanded this time period from 355 years to over 2,600 years. Assuming each generation lasts 36 years, then there would be 72 generations, such

[3] White, AJM (2010), *What About Origins?*, (Leominster: Day One Publications), p77

that for every generation listed, six are missing. If the writer of Genesis was so careless as to omit over 85 percent of the generations in Genesis 11, why did he waste time giving us the information in the first place? What purpose would it serve, since it would be so inaccurate?

These examples show the folly of accepting a creation event as distant as 10,000 B.C. Those who accept even longer ages have a worse problem; they must insert 10 to 100 times as many "missing generations" in Genesis 5 and 11 as those who hold to a creation of about 10,000 B.C. Interestingly, both camps loathe explaining where these missing generations are to be inserted. All they know for sure is that they are missing! Those who hold to the inerrancy of the Scriptures should reject all attempts to make the earth older than the Hebrew text warrants, which is about 4000 B.C.[4]

Andy McIntosh makes the same point as Pierce and Ham.

---

[4] Pierce, L. And Ham, K. (2008), *Are There Gaps in the Genesis Genealogies?* In Ham, K. (ed.), *New Answers Book 2*, (Green Forest, AR: Master Books), p61

Only by making the term 'begot' mean 'fathered the line leading to' could substantial gaps be argued for. But such thinking is tortuous, when the straightforward reading is plain and understandable and secondly, the overall thrust is so the reader may know who were the ancestors of Abraham/Noah and how long ago they lived.[5]

McIntosh's comment points the way to why this issue is important for the current discussion. It is important to believe that there are no gaps, so that we can see that Abraham was directly descended from Adam, and also that Jesus was directly descended from Adam. If we start with a presupposition that there are no gaps in the Genesis genealogies, then some remarkable facts stand out. If there are no gaps, then the numbers and ages quoted in these chapters can be used for simple arithmetic calculations of dates. For example, without gaps, we find that Methuselah's death occurred 1656 years after creation (1656AM – Anno Mundi, the Year of the World). Now Methuselah's name means "his death shall bring it".

[5] McIntosh, A. (2006), *Genesis for Today*, (Leominster: Day One Publications), pp48-49

We know that Methuselah's father, Enoch, was a prophet. Therefore, it would make sense to suggest that Methuselah's name was a prophecy for the dating of the Flood. Ken Ham has often remarked that people should have been nervous every time that Methuselah had a cold! Pierce and Ham again:

> Some Hebrew scholars believe that the name *Methuselah* means "when he dies it is sent," referring to the Flood. Assuming no gaps in the chronology, Methuselah died the same year the Flood began. Some Jews believed that God gave Noah time to mourn the death of Methuselah, whom they believe died a week before the Flood began (Genesis 7:4). If this is so, then no missing generations can be inserted here. If this were not the case, then this is the only place in Genesis 5 one might attempt to shoehorn the missing 22 generations! Would you trust a chronologist who was so careful to record names and ages yet omit 22 generations in his tabulation in one place? It simply doesn't follow.[6]

---

[6] *ob cit*

If you are not yet convinced, then please try this with me. Just assume for a moment that there are no gaps in the genealogy of Genesis 5. What Ken Ham and Larry Pierce and Andy McIntosh are saying is that, if we start with this assumption, then everything just works. The year of the Flood is the same as the year Methuselah died. Not only that, but have a look at the following diagrams.

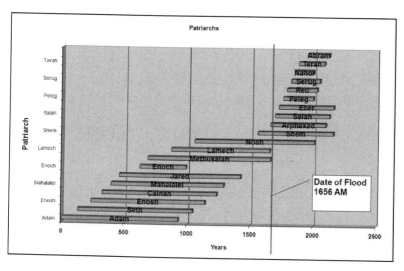

This first Excel chart shows that Methuselah's death is the same year as when the Flood came. It also shows that Lamech died before the Flood, predeceasing his father. Lamech's name means "weary". Indeed, the names of each of the ten antediluvian patriarchs are special, and combine to make something interesting - but this only works, if there are no gaps in the genealogy of Genesis 5.

Meanings of Patriarchs' Names	
Name	Meaning
Adam	Man
Seth	Appointed
Enosh	Mortal
Cainan	Sorrow
Mahalalel	God be praised
Jared	Shall come down
Enoch	Teaching
Methuselah	His death shall bring it
Lamech	Weary
Noah	Rest

Thus, the first ten patriarchs' names read as follows.

Man is appointed mortal sorrow, but the God who is to be praised shall come down, teaching that His death shall bring the weary rest.

So the "coincidence" of the names - which I take to be prophetic and coincidental at all - does not work if there are any gaps. Since the genealogy of Genesis 11 is of a very similar style to Genesis 5 - and different from other genealogies in the Bible, which do not contain numbers - we can assume that Genesis 11 does not contain gaps either. If this is so, we get the remarkable graph shown below, when we plot their ages at death against generation.

The ages of patriarchs before the Flood remains approximately constant - with two exceptions. Enoch did not die - he was taken away by God.[7] Lamech died

---

[7] This has happened to two people in the Bible - Enoch and Elijah. Since the bible teaches that men die once, and since Revelation speaks of two witnesses in the last days, there are many who suppose that the two witnesses of Revelation could be Enoch and Elijah. I have sympathy with this view. However, it should be noted that many other godly scholars - including many who work in the same ministry as myself - would propose different names, and for that reason, I will not dogmatically assert this suggestion, which must remain merely a suggestion.

at the extraordinarily early age of 777! (extraordinary for antediluvian times). I would suggest that his name

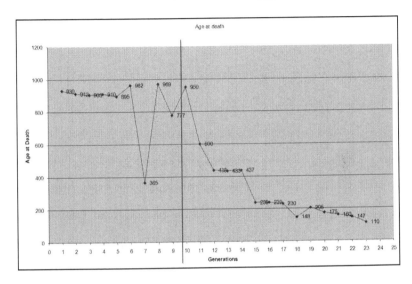

implies that he died early in fulfillment of prophecy. The curve of best fit for the post-Flood patriarchs is exponential in nature. Remarkably, the curve resolves at approximately 70 - and the Bible teaches that the average life span is "three score years and ten", or 70.

Abram Fits the Genealogy

So what has all this got to do with the life of Abram? Well, it puts Abram's ages and dates - and indeed those of his wife Sarah - into context. When we see the curve

Detail from a 1906 Bible card, from WikiCommons

of ages, we realize that Abram was not some sort of freak to live to the age of 175 - this age was the "correct" age for a man of his generation. Similarly, Sarah dying at an age of 127 would not be abnormal.

Many of the events of Abram's life have dates or ages attached to them. This means that the dates must be important. As we have seen, nothing is included in the Bible without significance.

One piece of information often overlooked - presumably out of modern distaste - is Sarah's relationship to Abram. Sarah and Abram were half-siblings, sharing the same father; Terah. (Genesis 20:12) At the time of Moses, such close relationships between husband and wife were forbidden. The reason for such marriages being forbidden is for our safety. Such close intermarriages bring genetic problems. The offspring are more likely to inherit genetic errors from their parents, as the errors will be similar. However, such a regulation could not be made in the immediate post-Flood world, both because of the lack of availability of other prospective partners, and the fact that the genetic errors - which must also have caused the decrease in longevity seen on the curve - would not have multiplied to a dangerous enough extent by the generation of Abram and Sarah. If the Flood had not been a worldwide event, then these issues would not have arisen, so the longevity curve and the ability for half-siblings to marry, without attracting censure from God, is actually good circumstantial evidence that the Flood was indeed worldwide, as the Bible says it was. So here we have an example of something in the life of Abram, which is difficult to understand if the first eleven chapters of Genesis are not literal, but which fits perfectly with a belief in Genesis 1 to 11.

There is, of course, more evidence. We need to look more closely at the ages of Abram and Sarah. We read that Abram was 75 when he left Haran. (Genesis 12:4).

We do not know when Abram, Sarah, Terah and Lot

$$\frac{75}{175} \times 70 = 30 \qquad \frac{65}{127} \times 70 = 35$$

had left Ur for Haran, but it could have been some years earlier. However, we do know that Sarah was ten years younger than Abram (Genesis 17:17), so therefore Sarah was 65 when they left Haran.

Suppose that the reason that Terah first left Ur was that God was speaking to him at that stage. His obedience was not complete. This was because Terah was a pagan, according to Joshua 24:2. This would also underline why Abram was told to leave his father behind (Genesis 12:1). Abram and Sarah would then have been living in Haran, during years when Sarah could have conceived a child. However, she did not conceive a child. Genesis 11:30 tells us that Sarah was barren. Her lack of reproduction was therefore a medical condition.

Now, most pictures of Abram leaving Haran show him as an old man. A 75-year-old would indeed be an old man today. But I find it difficult to believe that Abram would age "normally" to the age of 75, and then live for another 100 years. I think it is more likely that the aging process would be proportionately long for both Abram and Sarah. So, a little arithmetic will give us "modern-equivalent" ages for Abram and Sarah, at

the time they left Haran - assuming that their ages at death were "normal" for people of their generation. And that assumption of normality of their longevity is based entirely on an assumption that the genealogy of Genesis 11 has no gaps, and that the first eleven chapters of Genesis are true. With these assumptions, we see that Abram and Sarah, at the time of leaving Haran, were both equivalent to "modern ages" of early thirties. They were still a relatively young married couple, and still well within child-bearing age. The artist, Ben Scotton, has drawn the images shown of Abram and Sarah at this stage of their lives. The illustrations show them much younger than the earlier, more traditional picture of Abram, taken from Wikipedia Commons.

To understand the significance of Abram's journey to Canaan, we need to look back at where he had come from. Abram and his family had originally set out from Ur.

Ur was a city within the influence and orbit of Babylon, or Babel. Understanding the background to Babel is therefore important to understanding the background to Ur. I have written before on how the Tower of Babel was not necessarily a super-tall structure, but rather built in a manner "dedicated to the heavens" - i.e. dedicated to false gods.[8] With this in mind, we can see its dedication reflected in other apparently dissimilar structures around the world -

[8] Taylor, P. (2007), *The Six Days of Genesis*, (Green Forest, AR: Master Books), p203

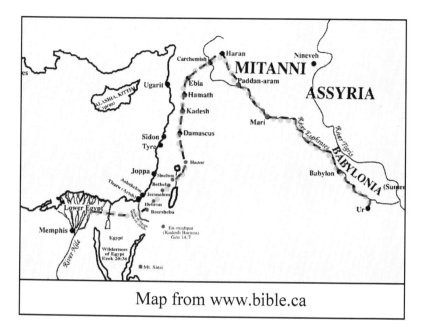

Map from www.bible.ca

such as Carnac or Stonehenge - which all have an astronomical, or more correctly astrological, purpose.

Ur had its own ziggurat, which can still be seen today. It was a rich and prosperous city, completely dedicated to paganism. Scotton's illustration, reproduced here, shows Abram with his father, Terah, and brother, Nahor, in a city where idols are being traded.

An initial glance at a map would suggest that Abram and his family were going the wrong way, when they journeyed from Ur to Haran. However, this is not so. To travel direct from Ur to Canaan would have been - and still is - very difficult. Most travelers would follow the fertile crescent, before turning southwards to Canaan. This is the route shown on the map. So when we understand the map correctly, we can see that Haran is actually *en route* to Canaan. This lends support to the idea that Terah was originally following God's instructions. There seems no other reason why it should be stated that they had all originally set out to go to Canaan (Genesis 11:31).

God's Promises in Genesis 12

Notice that the tense of the first phrase in Genesis 12 is the pluperfect tense.

Now the LORD **had said** to Abram... (emphasis mine)

This suggests again that the original instruction to leave Ur had been from God. In the following verses, God gives Abram a command and a promise.

"Get out of your country, From your family And from your father's house, To a land that I will show you. I will make you a great nation; I will bless you And make your name great; And you shall be a blessing. I will bless those who bless you, And I will curse him who curses you; And in you all the families of the earth shall be blessed." So Abram departed as the LORD had spoken to him, and Lot went with him. (Genesis 12:1-4)

The LORD told Abraham that he was to leave his country. Ur and Haran were his country. It was a country of wealth and power. Later information suggests that Abram was himself considerably powerful. Verse 4 shows that Abram obeyed this part of the command. However, the command went on to say that Abram was to leave his family and his father's house - meaning everything his father owned and was responsible for. Lot, Abram's nephew, was the son of Abram's brother Haran, who had probably already died by this point (Genesis 11:27). Lot was Terah's responsibility, because Terah had taken him on the original trip from Ur to Haran. Yet Abram took Lot with him when he left his father's family and house. Thus, Abram's obedience was not complete - it was tempered with a little disobedience. This element of disobedience would have serious consequences later on. Lot's children (by his daughters) gave rise to the nations known as the Ammonites and the Moabites. These two nations were to prove problematic to the Israelites later in history. Perhaps these nations would not have arisen, had not Lot been a thorn in Abram's side, and then had he not left to live in Sodom.

> And Abram was seventy-five years old when he departed from Haran. Then Abram took Sarai his wife and Lot his brother's son, and all their possessions that they had gathered, and the people whom they had acquired in Haran, and they departed to go to the land of Canaan. So they came to the land of Canaan. Abram passed through the land to the place of Shechem, as far as the terebinth tree of Moreh. And the Canaanites were then in the land. (Genesis 12:4-6)

This section of scripture suggests that Abram and his family were wealthy. They were taking a lot of possessions with them. They were also taking a lot of people. There were enough people to form a substantial army in Genesis 14. The KJV describes these people as "the souls that they had gotten in Haran". It might not be stretching the point to suggest that these people had become believers through Abram's witness in Haran, and hence they were the souls that Abram had gotten. God was sending them to the place where the Canaanites were. This land could not belong to the Canaanites, because all lands are God's to give. Moreover, the nation of Canaan was under a curse, as reported in Genesis 9:25. This curse would not affect everybody - any Canaanite who turned to God in repentance would be saved. One such was Rahab (Joshua 2:1), originally a Canaanite priestly prostitute, who not only joined God's people, but was a direct ancestor of Jesus (Matthew 1:5). The curse was in place for a reason, to give a wicked nation the opportunity to turn to God. The destruction of this people group was not immediate, and would only affect that number - unfortunately a large majority - who had not repented and believed in God. Therefore, when seen in this context, we see that the accusation, that the God of the Old Testament was into genocide and ethnic cleansing, is false.

At the terebinth tree, God delivered more of his promise to Abram.

> Then the LORD appeared to Abram and said, "To your descendants I will give this land." And there he built an altar to the LORD, who had appeared to him. (Genesis 12:7)

God promised Abram that he would have descendents. These descendents would become a nation, because only then would they be able to possess a land. This means that God was specifically promising a son. Consider again the state of Abram and Sarah. They did not have a son at this point, yet they were both young enough to have a son. Sarah was barren, which was why she had not had a son. Barrenness would have been something shameful at the time - an indication to those in Ur and Haran that Abram's deity was not looking after him, especially as many of the deities for sale would have been fertility deities. This promise, then, suggests that Sarah's barrenness was to be overcome. This in itself would have been a miracle, but maybe surrounding peoples would simply have attributed this to love potions, or incantations to fertility deities. God had an even greater miracle planned - and an important lesson. The lesson for Abraham was to have patience and faith, while Sarah was to pass well through the age of child-bearing, so that by the time Isaac was actually born, there would be no doubt that his birth would be a miracle.

Calvin puts it thus:

> Not only does he say that Abram was without children, but he states the reason, namely the sterility of his wife; in order to show that it was by nothing short of an extraordinary miracle that she afterwards bare Isaac... Thus was God pleased to humble his servant; and we cannot doubt that Abram would suffer severe pain through this privation. He sees the wicked springing up

everywhere, in great numbers, to cover the earth;
he alone is deprived of children.[9]

Abram built an altar to the LORD. It is significant that
his first act was one of worship. It was also an act of
sacrifice - an altar is a table on which sacrifices are
carried out, so verse seven suggests that Abram did
not come to God in his own strength, but only with the
covering provided by blood. The place of worship was
also to be significant, because Abram returned to this
very same spot, following his expulsion from Egypt, at
the end of that disastrous and disobedient episode of
his life.

Conclusion

The great themes that we have seen in the life of
Abraham can be expanded upon. We have seen that he
was a man of obedience and a man of faith. We have
seen that it was his faith that brought about his
salvation, not his actions. Therefore, Abram is the
supreme example of faith in the New Testament.

---

[9] Calvin, J. (1554), *A Commentary on Genesis*, (Edinburgh: Banner of Truth),
pp337-338

Romans 4 reminds us that Abraham was justified by his faith, not by his works.

> What then shall we say that Abraham our father has found according to the flesh? For if Abraham was justified by works, he has something to boast about, but not before God. For what does the Scripture say? "Abraham believed God, and it was accounted to him for righteousness." Now to him who works, the wages are not counted as grace but as debt. But to him who does not work but believes on Him who justifies the ungodly, his faith is accounted for righteousness. (Romans 4:1-5)

Galatians 3 reminds us of the same fact.

> Abraham "believed God, and it was accounted to him for righteousness." Therefore know that only those who are of faith are sons of Abraham. And the Scripture, foreseeing that God would justify the Gentiles by faith, preached the gospel to Abraham beforehand, saying, "In you all the nations shall be blessed." So then those who are of faith are blessed with believing Abraham. (Galatians 3:6-9)

There are so many books and articles that go into much detail on this aspect of the faith of Abraham. Many of them are worth reading. But, if New Testament faith looks back to Abraham, then we must also assert that it is difficult to understand his faith, without realizing that the events of his life depend on a background and foundation of the truth of Genesis 1 to 11. Abraham was of his time, and for his time.

The Second Coming of Jesus

Agreeing to Disagree

When I worked with *Answers in Genesis*, as a typical creationist ministry, it was noticeable that it has the following clause in its Statement of Faith.

> Jesus Christ rose bodily from the dead, ascended to heaven, and is currently seated at the right hand of God the Father, and shall return in person to this earth as Judge of the living and the dead.[1]

This is a very careful and measured statement of the position. It affirms that Jesus Christ will return one day in person. His return will be as Judge.

Most churches would need to say a lot more about the Second Coming of Christ. That is because there are a number of different viewpoints held by people who hold the Bible to be true. This is an important secondary doctrine and an individual church or a denomination will want to be clear exactly what they believe on the subject. The whole subject of Christ's

---

[1] Answers in Genesis Statement of Faith, Section 3 Clause 9, < http://www.answersingenesis.org/about/faith >

Return and the events surrounding the future is called *eschatology*. Many of the various eschatological positions are well known, and some people will assume that their position is the only correct position, and will be surprised that some people hold other positions.

AiG staff writer, Bodie Hodge, wrote an important article, explaining the criteria by which AiG judges that an issue is one on which AiG should take a position or not[2]. This is important, because many people today assume that we should be "tolerant" of other positions. They may wonder why AiG will be tolerant on issues such as eschatology but not on creation. Hodge explains:

> AiG is made up of Christians who unite to defend the authority of the Bible in today's secular culture. And that is what we are "on about"—the authority of the Bible, often in Genesis—a

[2] Hodge, B. (2009), *Where do we draw the line? - What it means to be a parachurch organisation*, < http://www.answersingenesis.org/articles/2009/10/19/where-do-we-draw-the-line >

foundational book, but also other places (like the gospel message of the New Testament).

Hodge goes on to explain that there are issues, on which AiG will comment, that pertain to the authority of scripture. His article gives a table of some of these - issues such as the Trinity, and other doctrines which appear in this book. In a second table, he lists doctrines which churches consider important, but where advocates of both sides of the argument are committed to the authority of scripture, and so the issue is one of interpretation, rather than biblical authority. Among these issues are Calvinism versus Arminianism, charismatic gifts and eschatology. Yet many people wish to relegate creationism to the same level. I recently agreed to appear in a video, published by the Faraday Institute, which is a theistic evolutionist organization, so that the position of creationism and biblical apologetics could be heard. In the biographical sketches of the accompanying book, my biography contains the following:

> Paul became a Christian in his early teens and was soon convinced of the scientific and historical

nature of the early chapters of Genesis. He has written four books and now frequently travels to speak on *this interpretation* of Genesis.[3]

It should be noted that this biography is partly copied from the Answers in Genesis website, except that they have made a mistake with my conversion age (**late** teens, not early), have removed my scientific qualifications and have inserted the words in the quote which I have italicized. Apart from that, it is perfect! However, one of the issues that I have been attempting to demonstrate in this book is that belief in a six-24-hour-day creation, as recorded in Genesis, is not an optional extra, but an important aspect of biblical authority, and that failure to accept the plain reading undermines biblical authority. Moreover, such a view is not an *interpretation* or Genesis - it is a plain reading. In this way it differs from people taking different eschatological positions, as their positions can rightly be described as interpretation.

---

[3] Bancewicz, R. (2010), *Test of Faith (Leaders' Guide)*, (Eugene, OR: Wipf and Stock), p118, emphasis mine.

The Second Coming and Biblical Authority

Having stated the issues regarding why holding different eschatological positions does not undermine biblical authority, we ought to analyze an important rider to this argument. Any theological position which denies the **fact** that Jesus is going to return **does indeed** undermine biblical authority.

Whether a Christian holds to a premillennial, amillennial or post-millennial view of scripture, believing in a pretribulation, mid-tribulation or post-tribulation rapture, he **must** believe that Jesus is definitely coming back again. We can therefore distinguish between the doctrine of the fact of the Second Coming and differing eschatological positions. The differing eschatological positions do not constitute an attack on biblical authority. Indeed, as the different camps pour over the scriptures, to back up their relative positions, the issue of biblical authority is actually strengthened. On the other hand, the truth of the doctrine of the Second Coming of Jesus **is** an issue of biblical authority.

For this reason, we can state that at least one eschatological position is, in fact, contrary to our position of biblical authority. That is the view known as Preterism. To be fair, there are some who hold what is known as a partial preterist view, and these people are not deniers of biblical authority. However, the full preterist view states that Christ has already returned and that the curse has now been removed. This view, which seems to fly in the face of reality (do they really believe the curse has been removed from this sorry world, in which we live?) undermines biblical authority, because it undermines the things that Jesus Himself said about His own return.

The Purpose of the Chapter

Having made these remarks, what would seem to be the point of a chapter in this book on the Second Coming? The thinking behind the book, we remember, is to establish that important Christian doctrines can be traced back to a foundation in Genesis. We have therefore examined the doctrines in the New Testament, in the Old Testament and finally their foundation in Genesis.

We have seen that parachurch organizations, such as Answers in Genesis, are best advised not to take a particular eschatological position. However, this injunction has also often transferred these days to churches. There is surely no harm in a church deciding on what their eschatological position should be. Moreover, the concern to tolerate other eschatologies often leads to preachers not approaching the subject of the Second Coming at all. Many younger people in our churches - particularly those under thirty - may never have heard a sermon on the Second Coming. This concern not to offend people means that the Blessed Hope, of which the scriptures teach (Titus 2:13) never gets taught, and Christians are robbed of the desire to look forward to Jesus' return.

For these reasons, it seems right to this author to tackle the subject. The problem is that in tackling the subject, I would probably reveal what my eschatological position is. Actually, anyone who has seen my personal website would probably already know what position I take. Rather than put people off,

I ought to be upfront and honest about my position, and show that those taking the other evangelical positions can equally trace the foundation of the doctrine of the Second Coming back to Genesis. It would be fine for a book to be neutral on this subject. However, there are a number of other creationist books which are not neutral on the subject - for example, John Macarthur's books, which are thoroughly sound on creation, take a dispensational premillennial position. Yet, when he is talking about the importance of Genesis, his arguments can be used, whatever one's view about the end times.

As I stated, it would not be difficult to ascertain that my own view of the end times is the position known as **Historic Premillennialism.** This view teaches that the thousand-year reign of Christ recorded in Revelation 20 is to be fulfilled literally. Historic Premillennialists suggest that the words of Jesus in Matthew 24 imply that Christians who are alive at the time will have to live through the literal seven-year period known as the Tribulation. After this, there is a simultaneous Rapture and Glorious appearing of Jesus, after which the afore-mentioned thousand-year reign happens. Finally, the devil is cast into the lake of fire, and God makes a New Heaven and a New Earth.

Dispensational Premillennialists agree with much of the above, but they maintain that Christ's return is in two phases, either side of the Tribulation. The Rapture of all Christians alive at that time happens before the Tribulation. Thus these two premillennial views of the end times are sometimes referred to as post-tribulation and pretribulation respectively. A third view - mid-tribulation premillennialism - is a branch of the dispensational view, except that they believe the Rapture will happen midway through the Tribulation, just before the second half of the Tribulation, which all three premillennial views know of as the Great Tribulation.

Post-millennialism suggests that the thousand-year reign will come before Jesus returns - i.e. the Second Coming will be "post" the millennium. This view expects the Gospel to be preached throughout the world with increasing effectiveness, until the return of Christ is brought in.

Amillennialism sees the numbers in Revelation as figurative. Strictly speaking, Amillennialism is a misnomer, as it implies that these people don't believe in the millennium. They do. Amillennialists take it that the millennium is simply the present period, between Christ's First and Second Coming.

The danger in listing these ideas so briefly is that those who hold a different view to me may already be cross with me, saying that I have misrepresented their view. If so, please refer to other descriptions of these positions. Two Historic Premillennialists, who have nevertheless catalogued all the views in more detail, are Wayne Grudem and David Pawson. References to their books are given[4,5]. Also, readers might want to read an easy-to-read commentary on Revelation, in each of the views. While I haven't been able to find an easy-to-read Postmillennial commentary, I have

---

[4] Grudem, W. (1994), *Systematic Theology*, (Leicester: IVP), pp1109-1139

[5] Pawson, D. (1995), *When Jesus Returns*, (London: Hodder & Stoughton)

referenced commentaries taking the other three positions.[6,7,8]

Having looked at the areas of disagreement, between Bible-believing Christians, on the issue of the End Times, we will now concentrate on the areas of agreement. The reason for this is that we will find that a failure to accept these areas of agreement will indeed result in an issue of biblical authority. These areas of agreement will be, therefore, not simply areas without contention in evangelical circles, but important lines in the sand for the true evangelical.

Boice has taken great trouble to catalogue these lines in the sand.[9] Among these are the reality of Christ's Return, the longing for Christ's Return, the final results of Christ's Return, the Day of Judgment

---

[6] Wilcock, M. (1991), *The Message of Revelation: I Saw Heaven Opened*, (Leicester: IVP). This commentary takes an Amillennial position.

[7] LaHaye, T. (1999), *Revelation Unveiled*, (Grand Rapids, MI: Zondervan). This commentary takes a Dispensational Premillennialist position.

[8] Ladd, G.E. (1972), *A Commentary on the Revelation of John*, (Grand Rapids, MI: Eerdmans). This commentary takes a Historic Premillennialist position.

[9] Boice, JM (1986), *Foundations of the Christian Faith*, (Leicester: IVP), pp705-713

and the Resurrection of the body. As has been our pattern, we will look for these doctrines in the New Testament, then in the Old and finally suggest their roots in Genesis. I will have to apologize in advance, if you think that any of my comments following are influenced just by my adherence to Historic Premillennialism, rather than by a commitment to scripture. It is the latter to which I aspire.

Christ's Return Mentioned in the New Testament

To list every possible New Testament mention of Christ's Return would make this chapter very long indeed, because His Return is one of the central themes of the New Testament. According to Boice, "one verse in twenty-five deals with the Lord's return. It is mentioned 318 times in the 260 chapters."[10] However, we have isolated a small number of facts about the Second Coming above, and it would be worth looking at a couple of scriptures, upon which our assertions of these facts are based.

---

[10] *ibid*, p705

I have heard it suggested - and believe it to be the case - that understanding Matthew 24 is the key to understanding all biblical prophecy, relating to the end times. I do not take a position that suggests that one part of scripture is more inspired than another, nor, like the so-called Red Letter Christians, assume that the bits printed in red in some Bibles - the words of Jesus - are more correct than everything else. Jesus speaks through the whole of scripture, because it is all inspired. That having been said, the fact that we have Jesus Himself speaking on the subject of His own return is not without significance.

At the beginning of Matthew 24, Jesus talks about the destruction of the Second Temple. His disciples assume that He is talking about the End Times. Therefore, they ask:

> Tell us, when will these things be? And what will be the sign of Your coming, and of the end of the age? (Matthew 24:3)

They assume that all these things are part of the same event. It must be stated that there are Christians

- the Preterists - who also assume that these events are one and the same, and that they happened in 70AD, so that there is no further prophecy to be fulfilled. Yet the world has clearly not ended yet. In fact, Jesus's answer shows that the disciples' question was really about three events.

1. The destruction of the Second Temple.

2. Christ's Return.

3. The End of the world.

In His answer, Jesus tells us that there will be false dawns - people who claim to be Christ returning, but who are not.

> Many will come in My name, saying, 'I am the Christ,' and will deceive many. (Matthew 24:5)

Having dealt with the counterfeit occurrences, however, Jesus makes clear that there will be a real return.

> For as the lightning comes from the east and flashes to the west, so also will the coming of the Son of Man be. (Matthew 24:27)

These words show us that Jesus was saying that He really will come back. This covers the **fact** of the Second Coming. But what about the **Longing**, the **Results**, the **Judgment** and the **Resurrection**?

In a sense, the longing for Christ's return is covered by the fact that the disciples even ask the question. This shows that they very much want Jesus to return. In His answers, Jesus' warnings about false Christs and false returns would not be quite so necessary if He did not want us to look out for His return. Part of His discourse includes the Parable of the Wise and Foolish Virgins. The Wise Virgins are commended for their preparation and their readiness.

> "Then the kingdom of heaven shall be likened to ten virgins who took their lamps and went out to meet the bridegroom. Now five of them were wise, and five were foolish. Those who were foolish took their lamps and took no oil with them, but

the wise took oil in their vessels with their lamps."
(Matthew 25:1-4)

So the watching and the readiness are covered.

Watch therefore, for you know neither the day nor
the hour in which the Son of Man is coming.
(Matthew 25:13)

This parable also refers to judgment. At the end of
the parable, the foolish virgins, who were not ready,
are excluded from the banquet, with these words:

Assuredly, I say to you, I do not know you.
(Matthew 25:12)

The concept of not being known by the Bridegroom
- that is, Christ on His return - is repeated in the
discourse about the sheep and the goats at the end of
Matthew 25. According to Matthew 25:31, these events
will happen "when the Son of Man comes in His glory".
The "goats", who are false converts, are given a
startling condemnation.

Then He will also say to those on the left hand,
'Depart from Me, you cursed, into the everlasting

fire prepared for the devil and his angels...'
(Matthew 25: 41)

This shows that there is a judgment, and that there are eternal results from Jesus' return. The Resurrection is explicitly mentioned, but is implied in the verses below. In the first quoted verse, many would see this as the rapture, rather than the bodily resurrection. If this were a book specifically on the Second Coming, I would comment on that, but for now we should restrict ourselves to noting that Matthew 24 and 25 imply a resurrection.

> And He will send His angels with a great sound of a trumpet, and they will gather together His elect from the four winds, from one end of heaven to the other. (Matthew 24:31)

> And these will go away into everlasting punishment, but the righteous into eternal life. (Matthew 25:46)

The five elements of the Second Coming that we have chosen to look for are also reported in the writings of the apostle Paul.

The Fact:

>...concerning the coming of our Lord Jesus Christ and our gathering to Him... (2 Thessalonians 2:1)

The Longing:

>We should live soberly, righteously, and godly in the present age, looking for the blessed hope and glorious appearing of our great God and Savior Jesus Christ. (Titus 2:12-13)

The Results:

>For God did not appoint us to wrath, but to obtain salvation through our Lord Jesus Christ, who died for us, that whether we wake or sleep, we should live together with Him. (1 Thessalonians 5:9-10)

The Judgment:

>The coming of the lawless one is according to the working of Satan, with all power, signs, and lying wonders, and with all unrighteous deception among those who perish, because they did not receive the love of the truth, that they might be

saved. And for this reason God will send them strong delusion, that they should believe the lie, that they all may be condemned who did not believe the truth but had pleasure in unrighteousness. (2 Thessalonians 2:9-12)

The Resurrection:

Behold, I tell you a mystery: We shall not all sleep, but we shall all be changed— in a moment, in the twinkling of an eye, at the last trumpet. For the trumpet will sound, and the dead will be raised incorruptible, and we shall be changed. (1 Corinthians 15:51-52)

There is much more can be said - a lot more from the words of Jesus and the epistles of Paul, as well as the epistles of Peter and John. However, this much will suffice to show the great emphasis the New Testament places on the facts and details of the Second Coming of Jesus.

Christ's Return Mentioned in the Old Testament

When I became a Christian, I assumed that Old Testament prophecy would be all about foretelling the first coming of Jesus. Of course, the Old Testament prophets had a lot to say on that subject. However, I was soon startled to discover that Old Testament prophecies also concerned the Second Coming.

The last few chapters of Isaiah seem at least to refer to the End Times. For example, there is a remarkable passage in Isaiah 65, which foreshadows phrases that appear in the book of Revelation. Certainly, the passage seems to be referring to the results of the Second Coming.

> For behold, I create new heavens and a new earth;
> And the former shall not be remembered or come
> to mind. (Isaiah 65:17)

Judgment is also mentioned in Isaiah. Take Isaiah 63, for example.

> Who is this who comes from Edom,
> With dyed garments from Bozrah,

This One who is glorious in His apparel,

Traveling in the greatness of His strength?—

"I who speak in righteousness, mighty to save."

Why is Your apparel red,

And Your garments like one who treads in the winepress?

"I have trodden the winepress alone,

And from the peoples no one was with Me.

For I have trodden them in My anger,

And trampled them in My fury;

Their blood is sprinkled upon My garments,

And I have stained all My robes.

For the day of vengeance is in My heart,

And the year of My redeemed has come.

I looked, but there was no one to help,

And I wondered

That there was no one to uphold;

Therefore My own arm brought salvation for Me;

And My own fury, it sustained Me.

I have trodden down the peoples in My anger,

Made them drunk in My fury,

And brought down their strength to the earth."

(Isaiah 63:1-6)

The last few chapters of Ezekiel, describing a new temple, also seem to be referring to the End Times. In his study bible, Jack Hayford suggests that "the temple is best interpreted symbolically, representing the worshipping community of the Messiah, during the church age, the Millennium and climaxing in the world to come."[11] While the comment may be influenced by Hayford's eschatology, most Christians would agree that the events referred to in Ezekiel 40ff have not yet been fulfilled.

It would be easy to use the prophecy of Daniel to proclaim a party line on the Second Coming, and it is perfectly fair for commentators to analyze Daniel in such a way. For the purposes of this study, however, we can see that Daniel 9 is certainly alluding to both the first and second coming of Jesus as Messiah.

> And after the sixty-two weeks Messiah shall be cut off, but not for Himself; And the people of the prince who is to come shall destroy the city and the sanctuary. The end of it shall be with a flood, And till the end of the war desolations are

---

[11] *The New Spirit-Filled Study Bible*, (Nashville, TN: Thomas Nelson), p1102

determined. Then he shall confirm a covenant with many for one week; But in the middle of the week He shall bring an end to sacrifice and offering. And on the wing of abominations shall be one who makes desolate, Even until the consummation, which is determined, Is poured out on the desolate. (Daniel 9:26-27)

Although differing interpretations will be made by the various camps about what the final week means, most agree that it is likely to be something to do with the events surrounding the Second Coming. Those from either the Historic Premillennial or Dispensational Premillennial camp are likely to interpret that final week as the Tribulation. But without going into that detail, we at least see that these prophecies concern the reality of the Second Coming, and indeed the longing for it.

One of the most remarkable Old Testament prophecies, referring to the Second Coming, is in Zechariah 14. Arguably, this passage not only shows the return of the Messiah, but implies resurrection, when we read that He will have "all the Saints" with Him (Zechariah 14:5).

> And in that day His feet will stand on the Mount of
> Olives,
> Which faces Jerusalem on the east.
> And the Mount of Olives shall be split in two,
> From east to west,
> Making a very large valley;
> Half of the mountain shall move toward the north
> And half of it toward the south.
> Then you shall flee through My mountain valley,
> For the mountain valley shall reach to Azal.
> Yes, you shall flee
> As you fled from the earthquake
> In the days of Uzziah king of Judah.
> Thus the LORD my God will come,
> And all the saints with You. (Zechariah 14:4-5)

We would not expect the Old Testament prophecies to be as clear on this subject as the New, but these few passages will at least demonstrate that we can arguably find all the elements of the Second Coming that we isolated above prophesied in the Old Testament.

Christ's Return Founded in Genesis

Answers in Genesis have frequently referred to the Seven Cs of History.[12] These provide a biblical framework for the whole of history, from the beginning to the end.

1. Creation

2. Corruption

3. Catastrophe

4. Confusion

5. Christ

6. Cross

7. Consummation

Looking at the diagram, there is a certain amount of symmetry observable. For example, the Cross is the

[12] See, for example, Ham, K., *The Seven C's of History*, < http://www.answersingenesis.org/articles/2004/05/20/seven-cs-of-history >

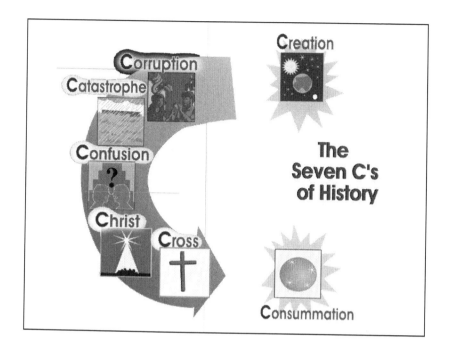

answer to the Corruption caused by the first sin. In the same way, there is a correspondence between Creation and Consummation. Those Christians who believe that Genesis is figurative believe that the world has always experienced death and disease. How, then, it must be asked, can they look forward to a world to come, in which there is to be no death or disease? The parallel is obvious. When we start by accepting Genesis 1 as actual history, we see that death is a temporary part of history. Death was not an original part of God's creation. 1 Corinthians 15 describes death as an enemy. We, therefore, have a more realistic hope of the final destruction of death.

It is small surprise, therefore, that many New Testament passages, referring to the Second Coming, allude to Genesis.

> But as the days of Noah were, so also will the coming of the Son of Man be. For as in the days before the flood, they were eating and drinking, marrying and giving in marriage, until the day that Noah entered the ark, and did not know until the flood came and took them all away, so also will the coming of the Son of Man be. (Matthew 24:37-39)

We have already seen that Matthew 24 is referring to Jesus' Return. In order to emphasize His return, Jesus compares His return to the time of Noah. This comparison would not make sense, if the account of Noah were not real.

The account of Noah tells us so much about Jesus. Hebrews 11 reminds us that the Flood is an image both of salvation and of judgment.

> By faith Noah, being divinely warned of things not yet seen, moved with godly fear, prepared an ark for the saving of his household, by which he condemned the world and became heir of the righteousness which is according to faith. (Hebrews 11:7)

The parallel between the Flood and the judgment at Christ's return is also seen in 2 Peter.

> For if God did not spare the angels who sinned, but cast them down to hell and delivered them into chains of darkness, to be reserved for judgment; and did not spare the ancient world, but saved Noah, one of eight people, a preacher of righteousness, bringing in the flood on the world of the ungodly....— then the Lord knows how to deliver the godly out of temptations and to reserve the unjust under punishment for the day of judgment. (2 Peter 2:4-9 - part)

It could be said that, in the events of the Flood, we see parallels with both the First and Second Coming of Jesus. We also see that Noah was a man of faith (Hebrews 11:7), saved by grace (Genesis 6:8).

In Hebrews 11:6, we read that Enoch - Noah's great-grandfather - was a man of faith.

> By faith Enoch was taken away so that he did not see death, "and was not found, because God had taken him";[a] for before he was taken he had this testimony, that he pleased God. But without faith it is impossible to please Him, for he who comes to God must believe that He is, and that He is a rewarder of those who diligently seek Him. (Hebrews 11:5-6)

The name Enoch means "Teacher", and we assume that he imparted his wisdom to the antediluvian people. He named his son, Methuselah, prophetically, because the name means "His death shall bring it", and Methuselah died the very same year that the judgment of the Floods came. We have another recording, however, of Enoch's prophetic words. The

Bible contains a quote from the book of Enoch in the epistle of Jude. This does not mean that the Bible endorses the book of Enoch, which is a non-biblical book. However, the inspiration of the Holy Spirit has therefore ensured that we can accept these words of Enoch as being true and prophetic.

> Enoch, the seventh from Adam, prophesied about these men also, saying, "Behold, the Lord comes with ten thousands of His saints, to execute judgment on all, to convict all who are ungodly among them of all their ungodly deeds which they have committed in an ungodly way, and of all the harsh things which ungodly sinners have spoken against Him." (Jude 14-15)

The most important foundational aspect of Genesis, with respect to the Second Coming and the End Times, however, is the expectation of a perfect world to come. Our world was spoiled by a literal sin that brought in death - both physical and spiritual. This death will be undone in the world to come.

> And God will wipe away every tear from their eyes; there shall be no more death, nor sorrow, nor

crying. There shall be no more pain, for the former things have passed away. (Revelation 21:4)

Because of Adam's sin, God cursed the world. This was a real historical event - and is paralleled by the removal of this curse in the world to come.

And there shall be no more curse. (Revelation 22:3)

There can be no realistic expectation of a perfect world to come, without there having been a perfect world in the past. And the New Heaven and New Earth to come will not take millions of years to evolve.

Conclusion and Summary

This has been a whistle-stop tour around some of the most important and significant Christian doctrines. The task that we set ourselves was to look at what the doctrine was, see where it occurs in the New Testament, then in the Old Testament and finally see how it is founded upon an acceptance of the truth of the early chapters of Genesis. While this book is nowhere near pretending to be a systematic theology, the diversity of the small number of doctrines chosen shows the truth of the statement that most, if not all, Christian doctrines are based on a foundation of the truth of Genesis.

Trinity

Understanding the Trinity is at the heart of understanding the nature of God. There is one God, but He is in three Persons. Each person of the Trinity is God and co-equal, but there is just one God. We saw that this was reflected in the language of Genesis. Although it would be hard to develop the doctrine of the Trinity from Genesis alone, once we have established it elsewhere from scripture, we see the doctrine reflected in the use of the plural Hebrew word *Elohim* for God with the singular word for *created*. We see the work of the Father, Son and Holy Spirit all in Genesis, as well as the insistence that there is only one God.

Deity of Christ

Jesus is seen to be both human and divine. He is not 50% God and 50% man. He is 100% God and 100% man. These two natures (in one person) are seen in Genesis, especially in the pre-incarnate human appearances of Jesus.

Inerrancy of Scripture

The importance of believing in the inerrancy of scripture is reflected in the account of the temptation of Eve by the serpent. We see how Satan attempted to create doubt, and to misquote scripture. We also see how he eventually directly contradicts scripture. In addition, we see the dangers caused by not being fully conversant with God's word, and, therefore, misquoting it, as Eve did in Genesis 3. It is a concern that so many churches today seem to be falling into this trap of misquoting scripture.

Sin and Death

Genesis is of vital importance to understanding the origins of sin and death. Even those theologians, who deny the literal truth of Genesis argue that it explains where sin and death came from. However, it is much easier to understand how these attributes came to pollute our world, if we accept Genesis as history. Moreover, we can see clearly how and why they will eventually be ended by God. A faulty view of the historical accuracy of the origins of sin and death in Genesis 3 leads to a faulty understanding of how sin and death will be finished with, in the world to come.

Doctrines of Salvation

Given that sin, and its consequence death, have polluted our world, and that those who have committed sins - which is everyone - deserves to be condemned by the Holy God to an eternity of hell, it is important to know how the doctrines of salvation find their roots in Genesis. It is notable that the first statement of the Gospel was given by God immediately after the first sin - and this fact underlines the love and mercy of God, as well as His holiness and justice. It was not possible to analyze all aspects of salvation, so we chose four doctrines - *atonement, grace, justification* and *sanctification*. In each case, they were shown to be based on a foundation of Genesis.

Abraham in Context

This chapter is slightly different from the others, concentrating as it does on aspects of the life of one person. However, Abraham is rightly held up as the great example of faith, and many commentators concentrate on the New Testament occurrences of the doctrine of faith as exemplified by Abraham. The purpose of this chapter was to show that we cannot fully understand this faith of Abraham, in Genesis 12 and following, without seeing his life in the context of the truth of Genesis chapters 1 to 11.

Second Coming

It is an important article of faith that this world will not be here forever. The world that God began, He will bring to an end. He will bring about a New Heaven and a New Earth, in which there is perfection and in which there is no death or curse. This chapter does not concern itself with the differing opinions on *how* this end will come about, but on the truth of the Second Coming, and how Jesus' return and the end times are best understood in the context of the truth of Genesis. It is noteworthy that fears of causing divisions over eschatology seem to be preventing many churches from preaching on the truth of the actual fact of Jesus' return. So churches are missing out on the first things and the last things of the Bible, which removes the message of the Gospel from all eternal context.

I started this book by lamenting the lack of seriousness with which people view doctrines and teaching. Biblical doctrines are exciting, and help us more fully to understand God and therefore more effectively to worship Him. Clearly, it is my desire to see people accepting the book of Genesis as truth, but this book has not just been about Genesis. We have seen how believing Genesis to be true affects the way we accept the rest of scripture and, in my opinion, underscores the truth of the rest of scripture. The Bible is one message. The Bible contains just one message of salvation. I hope this book greater enhances your appreciation and love of God's word. If it does, then I will have achieved my aim.

Bunyan's Commentary on Genesis

A Commentary on Genesis by the author of **Pilgrim's Progress**.

At the end of his life, John Bunyan was working on a commentary on the Bible. However, he only managed to get as far as Genesis 10 - and a little bit of Genesis 11. The commentary was published just a couple of years after his death, as part of a Complete Works edition. Another edition of the Complete Works was published in 1853 by George Offer, whose notes, like Bunyan's text, are long since out of copyright.

As far as we know, this is the first edition of the book to be published separately. As such, it is a beautiful book to own and to refer to.

The introduction and extra notes are by Paul F. Taylor.

Available from Just Six Days.

www.justsixdays.com

Have You Read Genesis Lately?

Well? Have you read Genesis lately? If not, why not get this book, which contains the complete text of Genesis? You could read it like a novel. Every chapter features at least one note, written by Paul F. Taylor.

Available from Just Six Days.

www.justsixdays.com

Letters to the Thessalonians
By Paul Taylor

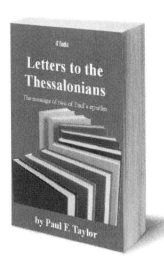

The two epistles to the Thessalonians contain much of the basic, biblical teaching on the End Times. For this reason, they have often been controversial. Yet the material they contain is essential for anyone who wants to get to grips with this subject, as well as providing an insight into the establishment of a church, which the apostle Paul commends as behaving exactly as a church should.

Paul Taylor argues that a literal reading of these epistles leads one to a Historic (Posttribulation) Premillennial understanding of the End Times.

Available from Just Six Days
www.justsixdays.com

Made in the USA
Charleston, SC
03 January 2016